Your

POETRY C·

GREAT MINDS

Your World...Your Future...YOUR WORDS

- Over To You
Edited by Steve Twelvetree

 Young**Writers**

First published in Great Britain in 2005 by:
Young Writers
Remus House
Coltsfoot Drive
Peterborough
PE2 9JX
Telephone: 01733 890066
Website: www.youngwriters.co.uk

SB ISBN 1 84602 218 5

Foreword

This year, the Young Writers' 'Great Minds' competition proudly presents a showcase of the best poetic talent selected from over 40,000 up-and-coming writers nationwide.

Young Writers was established in 1991 to promote the reading and writing of poetry within schools and to the youth of today. Our books nurture and inspire confidence in the ability of young writers and provide a snapshot of poems written in schools and at home by budding poets of the future.

The thought, effort, imagination and hard work put into each poem impressed us all and the task of selecting poems was a difficult but nevertheless enjoyable experience.

We hope you are as pleased as we are with the final selection and that you and your family continue to be entertained with *Great Minds - Over To You* for many years to come.

Contents

Kimberley Griffiths (11)	38
Adam Rees (13)	38
Becky Jones (14)	39
Justin Powell (13)	39
Charlotte Beynon	40
Hannah Francis (12)	40
Joseph Watkeys	41
Aimeé-Francis-Edwards	41
Charlotte Davies (13)	42
Rebecca Gillman (12)	42
Gabrielle Lewis (13)	43
Laura West (14)	44
James Lloyd	44
Stefanie Clark (14)	45
Lauren Sourbutts (14)	45
Arianwen Caiach-Taylor (13)	46
Molly Jones (14)	46
Natalie Rees (14)	47
Rhian Jones (14)	47
Victoria Griffiths (13)	48
Mirella Burgess	49
David Lewis (13)	50
James Thomas	51

Crown Hills Community College, Leicester

Dharmesh Patel (13)	51
Amardeep Singh (13)	52
Veena Patel (13)	52
Meera Bhanji (14)	53
Natalie Doughty (14)	53
Suraiya Jagot (13)	54
Tyler Boyce (14)	54
Carrie-Ann Bugby (13)	55
Nilesh Odedra (13)	55
Ali Madarbukus (14)	56
Kerry Byrnes (14)	56
Hardik Purohit (14)	57
Ashish Raja (13)	57

Kilsyth Academy, Kilsyth

Laura Muir (13)	58
Caroline Hood (11)	58
Katy McGlinchey	59
Amy Woods	59
Rachel McGale (12)	60
Shelly Bamford (12)	60
Hannah Boyce (12)	61
Emily Morrison	62
Stacey McMahon	62
Daniel Muir	62
Amy Stewart (12)	63
Marie Quinn (12)	63
Samantha Croal (12)	64
Victoria Marshall	65
Callum Holmes (13)	65
Carrie Jasmine Kaur Lota (12)	66
Matthew Thomson (12)	67
Gemma Butterly (12)	67
Andrew Fowler (14)	68
Jamie Turner (12)	68
Rebecca Fitzsimmons (12)	69
Emma Gray	69

Lockyer's Middle School, Wimborne

Tom Hunt (11)	70
Sharnie Mead (12)	70
Katherine Williams (11)	71
Thomas Joy (12)	72
Jennifer Bolton (11)	73
Amy Prewer (12)	74
Heidi Beasley (11)	75

Longton High School, Stoke-on-Trent

Brandon Hulme (12)	75
Abi Shubotham (13)	76
Natasha Harper & Louise Shaw (13)	76
Grant Cork (12)	77
Nathan Wilkinson	78
Nicola Johnson (12)	78

Natalie Dudley (13)	79
Jade Tinsley (13)	79
Lee Lovatt & Aaron Phillips (11)	80
Ben Dyke (13)	80
Rachael Lindop (13)	81
Craig Grestow (12)	81
Danielle Minor & Amelia Wiggins (12)	81
Kainat Rehmin	82
Heena Hussain (13)	82

Michael Hall School, Forest Row

Josh Holt (18)	83
Alexander Willink	84
Sara Doron (17)	85
Maddy Worsley (18)	86
Vanessa Odell (15)	87
Merle Hunt	88
Beth Pridham (15)	89
Rhiannon Lake-Edwards (16)	90
Abra Hunt	90
Stephanie Kerridge (16)	91
Euan Crowder (16)	91
Ben Holt (16)	92
Sapphire Allard (15)	92
Holly Westlake (16)	93
Jessica Bleach (16)	93

Priory School, Lewes

Louisa Taplin (13)	94

Rugby High School, Rugby

Harriet Mchale-Owen (12)	96
Emily Vincent (11)	97
Kayleigh Gray (13)	98
Megan Jacob (12)	99
Lauren Knights (13)	100
Lindsey Frodsham (13)	101
Ella Horne (13)	102
Hannah Gamble (13)	103
Ushna Qureshi (13)	104

The Cheltenham Ladies' College, Cheltenham

The Cherwell School, Oxford

The Neale-Wade Community College, March

The Poems

You Gotta Live For Today

I'm livin' for this hour, this minute, this moment
Because death will come in this second won't it?
Yesterday never happened and tomorrow will never find
I'm just living from 12 in the morning to 11.59pm.
So when it strikes 12 I'll be free from yesterday
because I might die tomorrow, maybe I died before today.
I need to show you how much these minutes mean
and how you need to savour those moments between.
A pillow's pressed on your face, do you need air?
A bullet's wedged in your heart, are you aware?
A deep trench in your wrist, did you feel it tear?
Go ahead, walk into a busy street, unaware,
Does that seem fair?
Is this a scare, that life can end without prepare?
Why does it matter, live here, not there.
Maybe that's all it takes to be gone,
did each of those actions take too long?
Maybe you need to visualise what I'm trying to convey
and realise the importance
of living for today.

Megan Edmonds (15)

Losing Grip/Falling Down

Something's dragging me down,
I wish that I could climb up,
Six feet under the ground,
Is where I want to wake up.
Away from life on the whole,
Away from all of this crap,
My mind is out of control,
Pretty soon it will collapse.

I can't stop thinking of death;
My one true love, that is, death,
Answer to all of life's grief,
Death is the long term relief.

Though I long to be happy,
Willpower's failing on me,
I just keep being dragged down,
Can't lift my face from a frown,
I always feel so alone,
Even when company's grown,
Maybe I've some love for life,
But I can't find it - I've tried.
Somebody help me *and quick*
I'm falling down - losing grip!

So when I've breathed my last breath,
When I've encountered death,
Remember that I did fall,
Was not a jump - but a fall,
I may have taken my life but,
Although my hand bared the knife,
Something was dragging me down,
It dragged me six feet under the ground!

Rosalind Bruce (14)

Friends Forever

A friend is someone who's always there,
Who gives advice, who really cares.
They'll take you shopping, sometimes up town,
They'll never ever let you down.

A friend is someone you love to have around,
Despite the bitter, but healthy rows.
You share your secrets, tell them all,
Exchange thoughts then hit the mall.

A friend is someone who's got you sussed,
Who knows how your mind works, someone you trust.
They know your darkest secrets, your deepest fears,
They're ready to comfort you when you're in tears.

Everyone has different fears, some nasty and some nice,
When you count your blessings, always count them twice.

Laura Tan (13)

Let Love Live . . .

Let love live in our veins,
Let love live in our hearts,
Let love live in our soul,
Let love live in our minds
But don't let love live on Earth.

For when love steps foot here, corruption shall attack,
Love is pure and will not fight back.

Love lives for peace, equanimity and innocence,
Let love live as the foetus,
Let love live all the time it's worth . . .
But don't let love live on Earth.

Leave love hidden in the complications of biology,
For the complexities of Earth shall bring pain and flood,
Let love live . . . only in our blood.

Sarah El Husseini (17)

The Rainforest

In the wet rainforest,
There are birds that fly free,
Native Indians,
And monkeys in the tree.

With tropical fruit
And trees with vines,
Dirty swamp lakes,
And mountains to climb.

Snakes that eat eggs,
And parrots eat seeds,
Jaguars eat meat,
And chimps eat leaves.

With humid conditions,
At day and night,
It's wet and sticky,
Insects come out to bite.

Some rainforests are getting chopped down,
People want to get lots and lots of money,
But animals are losing their homes,
Like birds, monkeys and wild bees with their honey.

So in some rainforests,
They are beautiful and bright,
But some others are getting chopped down,
It's a terrible sight!

Georgina Cosmedin Dunn

I Wish

I wish I was a Mars bar
All wrapped up nice and neat
So every time you took a bite
Your lips and mine would meet.

But when it was gone
How I would mourn
Until our lips would meet
So off he went with thirty-two pence
And the knowledge our lips would meet.

Wrap me up, wrap me up
All chocolatey and nice
Put me in your lunch box
So I'll be by your side.

And when you find me
In your lunch box
All wrapped up nice and neat
How glad you'll be
To find me
So our lips can meet.

Shanice Lockwood (13)
Airedale High School, Castleford

Red

A fire raging furiously,
The intense heat burning.
A drop of blood on rosy lips,
Like a flame, the life flickering.
And on that spot, to this day,
A trail of poppies lead the way,
To where that cabin once stood,
A cabin haunted by the smell of blood.

Rosie Wainwright (13)
Airedale High School, Castleford

The Young Hero

The young war hero strode briskly,
As his steps came he took them quickly.
Was going there, to sign his name,
He only thought about glory; but no pain.
Nine weeks later away he went,
Said his goodbyes and off he was sent.
Soon enough he was there in a trench,
Then he realised this war had a stench.
Always wet and cold; didn't have no sleep,
He bit his lip at night to help stop his weep.
His sergeant one day, pushed him to the front line,
He didn't dare shout, kick off, scream or whine.
With a big breath in, over he jumped,
Fire! Bang! Pain! And down he slumped.
A week later back at home,
The hero's wife sits alone.
Her hands trembling as she reads the letter,
At least he's in a place that is better.
Where machine guns spit bullets no more,
No thunderous booms shake the floor
And artillery shots don't light the sky.
However, don't forget that love doesn't die,
One day his wife will join him too,
In that eternal place where no one is blue.

Sally Bennett (13)
Airedale High School, Castleford

Red!

A blazing fire
Raging flames
A pool of blood
A warm summer's day
An exploding volcano
A face of fury.

Theresa Begley (13)
Airedale High School, Castleford

My Animals

I have a lion cub, a little lion cub
She controls my favourite place - the dance studio
She dances energetically, but she gently roars if she's pestered.
She teaches and learns most of the time
Her face looks happy, lively, without a care in the world
I call her Sarah - my dance teacher.

I also have a hyena
She plays all day and lives life to the max
She's loud and giggly - lively and bouncy
She's the best pick-me-up when you're down
A happy and wacky kind of girl
Her innocent face makes you wonder
If she has a mischievous side
But when she smiles, all is told
Because that's when the hyena comes out to play
I call her Lauren - my 8-year-old sister.

I have the nicest dog in the world
A real goddess she is
Sometimes though, her bark is worse than her bite
She goes to work, then comes home and protects us
While rushing round all the time
Rush, rush, rush,
Apart from that
She's loyal and friendly
She's my best friend
I call her Mum.

Leanne Kirby (13)
Airedale High School, Castleford

My Street

My street is long and winding,
With detached and semi-detached houses.
In my street there are lots of kids,
But lots of the older generation too.

There are people who come to this school,
There are people too old to work.
There is Mathew and Joseph,
There is Mrs Grey and my grandma in my street.

Through my bedroom window, this is what I hear,
Children running around the street
And cars speeding by
This is what happens on my street.

Through my bedroom window,
This is what I see,
A block of Airedale High
And a lamp post lighting up
My street.

Nathan Fozzard (12)
Airedale High School, Castleford

My Street

The view from my window is all but bad,
Where the children are happy and all but sad,
Sarah shouts, while Laura will laugh,
Gemma is dancing while Clarissa acts daft,
All you can hear is the sound of rain,
Water running down our drain,
But the street is happy and everyone's out
With the odd person drinking or the odd lager lout,
Our street is good and a great place to live
Where everyone gets on and learns to forgive.

Terri Woolford (13)
Airedale High School, Castleford

Take Me Away

I cut my wrists and craved you more
I cried all day and locked my door
I begged and pleaded to get you back
You threw me out and made me pack
It was only a kiss, no passion or love
This wouldn't have happened if I pushed and shoved
Now I need you, I can't live alone
I know you paid the rent, but it was my home
Your child is mine, but you still took him away
Now I have nothing, I can't make it through the day
I need you with me, my world's at its end
I don't want to leave or be your friend
I shouldn't have done it, I shouldn't have touched
But they can't take me away, I love you too much
I'll make it up to you, but I don't know how
But I need you here with me
I need you back now.

Zoey Tibble (14)
Airedale High School, Castleford

Feelings Aren't The Case

Don't talk to me
I won't listen.
Don't question me
I won't speak.
Don't touch me
I won't feel.
Don't show me
I won't see.
Don't feed me
I won't taste.
Just kiss me
I'll embrace.

Laura Barker (13)
Airedale High School, Castleford

Knife

The knife struck deep,
Down into being,
It cut you away,
Without care,
Without seeing.

It matters not,
How much I deny,
It changes little
To refuse to cry.

The past remains
And cannot return,
Time spins ever on,
Despite how I yearn.

Mortality is a sentence
We are prisoners for life,
Never knowing when or where,
We may be struck by the knife.

Emma Hughes
Airedale High School, Castleford

Haikus

Autumn
Leaves all around you
Crispy underneath your feet
Red, yellow and brown.

Friends
Have a special bond
They help you when things are bad
Together always.

Jade Dickinson (12)
Airedale High School, Castleford

Friends?

Leaning back against the wall
I catch your eyes slowly fall
And in my mind it floats away
Drifting off to better days
And I know just how you feel
When it all just seems so real
There's no denying what is true
It's just something people do
And if the train should jump its tracks
Or if someone stabs your back
You know who's your best friend
From the start until the end
A million miles, a thousand days
I'll be right here with no delay
We all need someone from time to time
I got yours and you got mine.

Aimee Redman (15)
Airedale High School, Castleford

My Love For You

My love for you is like a rose
Each time you touch me it grows and grows
My love for you grows deeper and deeper
When I'm not with you I get weaker and weaker
My love for you I can say
I love you more than words can explain
Your smile is like the sun
It glows up all the words
Your eyes are blue just like the sky
Each time you hold I want to cry
Not because I hate, but because I love you
My love for you will never die.

L Parkinson
Airedale High School, Castleford

Muffassa

He's a cute little cat with an attitude
He'll drool all over you with his stinky breath.
And be your best friend when he's in the mood!
Females are attracted to him like magnets
That's why he begs at the door, 'Oh do let's!'

Oh the pain he went through when he was young
(It's surprising that he is so sweet!)
They chopped off so many bits he's glad that he's still got his tongue!
He has a lovely colour which is silver-grey
And looks more gorgeous every single day!

Apart from his past he's hardly ever ill
He's a cheery little boy no matter what
And he sometimes falls asleep on the window sill
He *can't* give us any lip
And from him you won't hear a pip!

Some people say he has been spoilt rotten
I don't think we can stop; we love him very much.
Though his food could feed a thousand men
He's a sweet little cat through and through
Muffassa I love you and I hope that you love me too!

Shanelle Bateman (12)
Airedale High School, Castleford

Haiku

Autumn
Colourful leaves fall,
Swirling in the calm, cold wind,
Bare, brown, leafless trees.

Lauren Guest (13)
Airedale High School, Castleford

Rapunzel

The story of Rapunzel is very different to the tale,
It started in a gale.
Rapunzel's mum and dad were in a cabbage patch,
When suddenly a witch (the owner of the cabbage patch)
                                                    lifted the latch.
'How dare you come onto my land,
I will turn you to sand!'
'No, no! Please do not lead us to slaughter,
To save our life we will give you our smelly daughter.'
So the witch took their daughter and locked her in a tower,
Everyone called the girl Smelly Rapunzel because she never
                                                    took a shower!
The years went by until Smelly Rapunzel was eighteen,
All the time she thought the witch was very mean!
Smelly Rapunzel waited at a window for her true love,
In that time she made a friend, a dove.
At last my true love has come!
I hope he isn't dumb.
'I have come to rescue you,
With my lasso.'
The knight threw his knife in the air,
But accidentally chopped off Smelly Rapunzel's hair!
He then threw his lasso
And chopped Smelly Rapunzel's head off too!

Zarina Earnshaw (11)
Airedale High School, Castleford

Paw Marks

There are paw marks on the table,
There are paw marks on the chair.
There are paw marks in the hallway,
As well as up the stairs!

There are paw marks in the bathroom,
There are paw marks on the mat.
There are paw marks on the aftershave -
Dad won't think much of that!

There are paw marks in the bedroom,
There are paw marks in the bed.
There are paw marks on my nightie,
In several shades of red.

Now, each and every paw mark
Came from a bear named Sid -
And all because the finger paints
Were left without a lid.

Bethany Sanderson (12)
Airedale High School, Castleford

Ebony

A CD player
Singing to itself.
Lyrics of a song
Hurting within.
Scars on her wrists
Bleeding with fear.
A small piece of paper
Lay by her side.
Full of words
Words full of hate.
'This is it, I have gone,
Goodbye, evil world.'

Katie Wilby (13)
Airedale High School, Castleford

The Jungle

In the jungle dark and deep
All the animals never sleep
There's a big baboon
And a lovely lagoon
Leading to the lagoon is a crocodile
And there's the river Nile
There's a cave of cats
And a load of black bats
In the cave there's a cheetah
Who always runs a metre
There's a pouncing puma
Who has a sense of humour
There's a losing lynx
Who can't swim and sinks
There's a reptile bush
That looks like mush
In the jungle there's eagle peak
And the eagles always seek
There's elephant mountain
What's always shoutin'.

Ashley Preval (12)
Airedale High School, Castleford

About My Person

Black combat trousers
Nothing in every pocket.
Red top with black sleeves
Weird logo on the front.
Green Day album
Empty - only words booklet.
CD player
Still playing the Green Day CD.
Eyeliner
On eyes but worn down.

Sophie Harvey (13)
Airedale High School, Castleford

The Shadow

The shadow is blackness,
Lurking in the corner,
Hear the sounds it makes,
Watch it getting stronger,
Rip you into flakes,
Scratch your insides out,
The only thing you can do
Is shout, shout and shout.
The shadow is darkness,
No looks of terror on its face,
People keep disappearing,
Police on the case,
The only thing you can do
Is hope through and through
For it to go away
But it could always stay.
The shadow is dead
Wanting flesh and blood,
Hangs around at night
Attacking things it could
Gives people a fright
Then takes them away
Now it stays.
The shadow is visible,
Looking back at you
The word is not miserable
Only scared will do.
Cannot run
Cannot hide
Caught in the eyes
Of the monster with pride.

Chloe Potter (11)
Airedale High School, Castleford

Holiday

The time has come to say goodbye
To a sunnier place I must fly
The thought of golden sands and sea
Is worth a million pounds to me
Across the sea is a magical land
Wherever you want it to be
From the Mediterranean to Afghanistan
From the clutches of English weather
To a place where never ends the summer
A glorious sunset, dancing in the night
The thought of home is such a fright
A ride on a train to Barcelona
Down the coast to Estepona.
A camel ride to the Isle of Capri
Wonderful memories of wonderful places
Lovely people with smiling faces
Then it ends, we're back in England
Oh my goodness, it's raining again!

Michael Gill (13)
Airedale High School, Castleford

Beastly Fire

Oh mighty beast
With all your might
Why, you put up a brilliant fight!
The red-hot flame
Feel no shame
Breathing fire
Is your desire
Oh mighty beast.

Kerry Etherington (12)
Airedale High School, Castleford

The Arctic Fox

The Arctic fox on the prowl,
Listen up, hear it howl,
There it is, white as snow,
Look around, it might not show.

Now it's summer, there it goes,
Take off the white coat
And let the brown show,
That's the Arctic fox, in summer and snow.

Melissa Hair (11)
Airedale High School, Castleford

The Monster Lurks

The monster lurks,
All about,
The monster lurks,
In and out,
The monster lurks,
But does not shout,
The monster lurks,
But then leaps out.

Jessica Moody
Airedale High School, Castleford

White

Angels in Heaven
The light at the end of the tunnel
Fog on a winter morning
The clouds in the sky
Smoke from a dying flame
The first snowflake of winter.

James Arnold (13)
Airedale High School, Castleford

About Their Person

A laptop in a briefcase
Rifling through cyberspace.
Converse sneakers
Growing weaker.
An MP3-player playing a song
No one can hear it, they're all gone.
The end nears
Silence falls
The night draws in.

Lauren Dalby (13)
Airedale High School, Castleford

A Recipe For A Perfect Day!

Begin with bags full of fun
Add a dash or two of sun
A packet of blue skies
Then pour in a bag of creamed ice
Fold in some happy faces
Mix in some cool places
Add a pinch of nice things to say . . .
And voilà! The perfect day!

Kiera Whitworth (13)
Airedale High School, Castleford

Hope

Hope is the last thing we think of at night,
Hope is the wish we pray for as we hug our pillow
And hope to sleep tight.
Hope is the bright light that brings me delight
Hope is the first flower that blooms in the spring
Hope is a feeling I feel deep within.

Chloe Bamford (12)
Airedale High School, Castleford

Life

Life is like a river flowing,
Where it goes
No way of knowing.

Life is like stepping stones,
Which one next
You choose alone.

Life is like a fire burning,
Get hurt by it
Carry on learning.

Life is like a wall being built,
Build it wrong
Fill with guilt.

Matthew Bradley (12)
Airedale High School, Castleford

Sheepwalk Lane

Every-sized houses, big and small,
But nearly everyone detached.
All different in their own way,
Stretching down the long main road.

There's Tony who can't hear the noise
And Anne who teaches young girls and boys.
Emma, whose smile is warm and friendly
And Mick who gardens tenderly.

The sound of cars driving past,
Fields stretching far and wide.
Flowing water in the pond,
Houses, behind trees, trying to hide.

Hannah Cook (13)
Airedale High School, Castleford

Keep With Reality

Open my eyes to this misty view of life,
True thoughts of confusion.
Shadowing the deepness of my pointless knowledge,
Finding happiness in a darkened room.

Trapped in loneliness, guiding me, leading me,
Keeping me somehow safe.
Not daring to be known or to shine through the jealousy or pain,
Destined to be different.

Walk each day trying to get the simple things right,
Shout in my face once more.
No prayers are answered for the innocent and pure,
No hope for the worthless.

Whisper sweet songs to me as I cry,
Clearing my mind from reality.
I know the pain, I live the pain you'll never understand . . .
How worthless, different, yet happy I am.

Sarah Hall (14)
Airedale High School, Castleford

The Horse's Dream

The brown, shining horse galloping across the field
Like lightning riding up to the long green fence
Where he saw a girl stroking his head
Where she was stroking, it tickled so finely
And I jumped over the long green fence.
I come to a wall, over the wall,
I saw miles of fields
Where I dreamt most nights
Of the little girl that I left many years ago
Where the wind's blowing
And the sun was shining
That is where I'll be going.

Chantell Cockerham (13)
Airedale High School, Castleford

Phoenix

You've felt your heart implode
A black hole, draining
Life from your cheeks,
Light from your eyes.
Preventing you seeing the world
As you should, with a child's joy.
Where your hope once lay
Is now an ashen wasteland,
Scorched by disappointment.

Yet do not despair my friend,
The end is never the end.

I once felt the same as you
I once had my heart dashed upon rock.
I had merged into my surroundings
And had reached the doors of Hell.
With Cerberus snapping at my heel,
Then I was rescued by a hand,
Similar to the one I offer now,
I was freed from the quicksand.

So do not despair my friend,
The end is never the end.

You see, some things happen,
Things we cannot control.
But life does go on
You may not see it now
But it's true, great phoenix.
Sometimes you just need an anchor
To keep you from drifting too far,
This one's in the shape of a friend.

So take my hand
And rise again.

Simon Lyall (18)
Banff Academy, Banff

If Only

If only you could see
What you're doing to me
If only you could see
What your hands do to me
If only you could see
The bruises you give me
If only you could see
The hurt you cause me
If only you could see
The pain I go through
If only you could see
The tears in my eyes
If only you could see
How you make me feel
If only you could see
How those names hurt me
If only you could see
Me telling you to stop
If only you could see
What your bullying does to me.

Rachel Shearer (15)
Banff Academy, Banff

Freedom

Freedom is why people try.
Freedom is why people cry.

Freedom is why the world goes round,
In the heart, is where freedom is found.

Freedom is not being told what to do,
Freedom is doing what is right for you.

Freedom is like a bird in the sky,
Freedom is like a car flying by.

Freedom's not found in a sword or a gun,
Freedom is found by having fun.

Freedom is why people strive,
Freedom is what keeps us alive.

Freedom is like a deer on a hill,
Freedom is space to do what you will.

Bobby Stewart (12)
Bearsden Academy, Bearsden

The Sea

Everyone talks about the Big Blue,
Even the animals that live in it too.
Everyone likes to play on land,
Especially when it is in the silky sand.

The beautiful water, so crystal clear,
Making a sound in your ear.
The crash of the waves on the shore,
The sound of the birds as they soar.

The sun goes down and everyone leaves,
They pack their things and put in their keys
And wave goodbye to the sea.

Carlos González-Campos (14)
Bellver International College, Mallorca

Sky-Skipper

The burning brightness
In the crisp clear sky
The scorched stronghold
Our great flaming eye
It is our sky-skipper

It is the golden orb
That gives us light
A shining hero from the east
Keeps us from fear and fright
It is our sky-skipper

The stallion in the sky
Searing across the world
Galloping across the heavens
Leaving a trail of burning light in its wake
It is our sky-skipper

The jewel in the crown of clouds
Sits gleaming above the world
Like a giant blazing ruby
With its rays of bewildering light
It is our sky-skipper

The flaming chariot disappears to the west
Come to the end of its daily quest
But the sky-skipper will return
So that its Earth may sizzle and burn
In the heat of our beloved sky-skipper.

Josh Bowles (14)
Bellver International College, Mallorca

The Sea

Roaring at the feet of windswept cliffs,
Lapping the bows of shore-bound ships,
Churning a broth of clear white froth,
Seamen at the mercy of its mighty wrath.

Galloping horses heading onto the sand,
Crashing onto land like a big brass band,
Flowing back into the gaping blue mouth
And smashing back on the cliffs of the south.

From the turbulent waves of the English coast,
To the turquoise-blue of which Caribbeans boast,
From the icy ocean of the Arctic north,
To the tranquil harbour where great ships berth.

The royal creature that covers the Earth,
Its regal head crowned with violent surf,
The tidal moon drags it onto the land,
Until chased away by the drying sand.

Tom Smith (14)
Bellver International College, Mallorca

The Competition

Sport of the finest, to the best athlete
They compete with their hands, play basketball
All gather in one place to meet and compete
They compete with their feet and play football.
To win, to be the best and not tire
Some sports may need you to glide like a strong rock
Some to jump longer, rather than higher
Such as a shot-put or badminton
To be the best, be strong, you must pedal.
You want to see the greatest colour - gold
Blood shall shrivel through to reach that medal.
Keep that weight up, don't let go, just keep hold.
You've reached your limit, tried your best
Now look at the sport score to see the rest.

Scott McInnes (14)
Belmont House School, Whitecraigs

Football Fantastic

When the ball goes to the back of the net,
All the fans get up off their seats and scream.
It flies through the air like a speeding jet,
The player prepares as if it's a dream.
The game, always played at a steady pace
The crowd gets excited when their man scores.
Champions are the winners of the race
We love to hear all the cheers and the roars.
Quitters don't win and the winners don't quit
The strength of mind and body means so much
The players, proud with the dirt on their kit
To score a goal with the final touch.
All the winners including the bosses
Aren't prepared to put up with losses.

Jared Ross (14)
Belmont House School, Whitecraigs

Music

Music, how I love to play the guitar
I am learning to play the piano
Some Indians like to play the sitar
There is a very similar tempo.
I love to listen to jazz instruments
Eric Clapton is a god of rock music
Music goes up in lots of increments
Hendrix was a god, he knew all the tricks.
A main part in a band is the lead bass
The rhythm is always played by the drums
The drums and bass, keep the rhythm and pace
The drummer and bass player use their thumbs
I have played the guitar in a duet
But I prefer to play in a quartet.

Hamish Dobbie (14)
Belmont House School, Whitecraigs

Life On The Streets

Life on the streets is like a puzzle, what's happening?
Shots being fired, people dying, lying in a big heap.
People in a huddle discussing why this is happening.
But why are people being admired for this deadly undoing?
Helpless people are hiding in corners, watching the days going,
Punches being thrown, people are depressed, can't go on now.
People finding innocent people, oh no, it is very sad,
Innocent people are worn now, don't know what to do.
These thugs are taking people's lives for granted but why?
Muggings are taking place in the streets all the time,
Bugs are being spread causing more problems in the streets.
Those on the streets, weep and cry for help now,
Life on the streets is not all that you think,
Some of the people are about to sink and go.

Max Modlin (13)
Belmont House School, Whitecraigs

Over The Top

Hello Fear, my old friend, back here to haunt me
Stuck in this miserable, wet, cold dyke
The Reaper comes so fast, I cannot flee
Death looms above, a storm, waiting to strike
Every night you visit and pick at my will
Fear, are you the herald of my demise?
It is all the same, to be killed or kill
It is a game, with life being the prize.
'Arm!' yells the Captain. 'It's you or them boys!'
The sun rose, the last I am likely to see.
I did this as a boy, but with safe toys
No time for fear, it was now one with me.
Fear wells up, like a balloon ready to pop
Dragging it with me, on, *over the top*.

Paul Morton (13)
Belmont House School, Whitecraigs

Food And Its Effect On Our World

Food, food everywhere; pizza, pineapple, pie,
Without it all we would be at a loss.
Without it all we would all suffer and die,
But all of this just has to have a cost.

Millions of people are always dying,
Children, adults and animals are under threat,
Corporate companies are always lying,
The civil riots one mustn't forget.

But the problem is in our heads, banging,
People donating to help the really poor,
Children lined up with their piggy banks clanging,
Send the NHS in, they'll help for sure!

So keep it in mind when you eat a big plum,
People die each year because they have none.

Rory Porteous (13)
Belmont House School, Whitecraigs

Love

Love is like the wind, it comes and goes,
Time passes and the seasons change.
Who knows if you will win or lose,
Will love be within your range?
Lonely days and dark nights,
I catch the wonders in a glimpse of an eye,
Till you reach that mountain of great heights,
Shimmering better than the clear blue sky.
Dropping down from my eye like a tear of joy
Peace as the ducks dance in their paddles.
Stop playing my heart as if it were a toy,
Then there you stand upon the green grassland,
Then suddenly you fade beside the stream,
I wake up, it was a dream.

Scott Greaves (14)
Belmont House School, Whitecraigs

Daydreaming Over Homework

As I look out the door of passing time,
I see the rain roll down the thick, glass pane.
My mother's moan goes on just like a whine -
To finish what I was doing again.
As it wastes away, the glass fills with steam,
The rain rolls down the pane - no different.
You feel yourself drift off into a dream
But there is one minor predicament.
The homework, clear as mud, due tomorrow,
Not a thought on what to do all around.
Better things to do fill you with sorrow
Why even do it - all my thoughts compound.
A better way to get work diminished,
Is to concentrate and get it finished.

Greig Paul (13)
Belmont House School, Whitecraigs

Before, During And After

A gentle wind blows through the dry, dry leaves
They cry out for water, so desperate and needy
Rustling grasses move in the breeze,
When the heavens open, they drink so greedy.
The heavens open and relieve the burden within
The grey sky cries torrents of tears.
It soaks the fat, the ugly and the thin
Making the small animals cringe with fear,
The heavens close and the tears stop.
A rainbow appears like an upside-down grin
All you can hear is the drip, drip, drop.
The sun peeks out, so slender and thin,
The water is gone, all is dry.
The plants and the animals wait for the skies to cry.

Sean Adair (13)
Belmont House School, Whitecraigs

Poverty

Money makes the world go round, or so they say.
Debt fills people with terrible dread,
And they just can't pay
So they can't sleep when they go to bed.

Mortgages and bills creep in around their ears,
The payments they just can't fathom.
Their hopes are being replaced with fears.
They feel like they're in a chasm.

The G8 don't seem to care
For the people who sorely need help.
They would rather figure out what to wear,
Than listen to the people who yelp.

'Help, help, save us,' we pray
Before our lives are taken away.

Fraser Murray (14)
Belmont House School, Whitecraigs

Lightning

L ightning, the shiny stuff that comes with thunder
I n the sky it makes a blunder
G reat white cracks appear in the sky
H iding under bedclothes, boys and girls cry
T errified pets run for their homes
N ever frightens the garden gnomes
I t cracks and pops with its ghostly glow
N earby trees in the wind they blow
G rowing weaker with every flash, I'm glad I made a quick dash.

Sophie Hughes (13)
Bryngwyn Comprehensive School, Llanelli

The Summertime

T he hazy, lazy days of the summer rush past like a train racing to
   its destination,
H alf the days are spent with people daydreaming and wishing,
E very so often the sun will go for a break and, instead, the ferocious
   rain clouds appear,

S un, shopping and relaxation are all the summer is recognised for,
U nder the hot, scorching sun, all types of fascinating creatures
   gather,
M others cast glancing eyes at their children who are busily playing
   in the park.
M owing lawns and barbecues are all the summer is good for,
E very single child is jumping for joy as school has finished
   until autumn.
R emaining sadness is cast aside and forgotten as happiness shines
   from every angle,
T ogether children stand catching butterflies and holding hands,
I nteresting flowers bloom as the sun picks out their beauty and
   stunning array of colours,
M oaning about the winter remains forgotten until it returns once more
   when winter comes again,
E nding so pleasantly but there is another year until summer brings
   happiness into lives again.

Amy Richards (14)
Bryngwyn Comprehensive School, Llanelli

Great Minds

Great minds think alike,
Come up with the best ideas,
Great minds think a lot,
When it comes to the crunch,
Great minds think all day
And discover great things,
How I would like to have a great mind.

Laura Evans (14)
Bryngwyn Comprehensive School, Llanelli

Buffy Alphabet

A is for Angel, the first vampire with a soul,
B is for Buffy, who's one kick-ass slayer,
C is for Cordelia, popular and cool,
D is for Dawn, too young to know,
E is for evil, there's a lot in the world,
F is for Fred, standing brave and tall,
G is for Gunn, kill first, ask questions later.
H is for Hellmouth, that sits under the high school,
I is for information that Giles gathers to win,
J is for Jonathan, once a superstar,
K is for Kennedy, a new potential slayer,
L is for Lorne, he can see right through you when you sing,
M is for mortals whom the Scoobies save,
N is for nasty, that's what the demons are,
O is for Oz, cool and calm,
P is for Potentials, they wait to be called,
Q is for Quentin Travers, at the Watcher's Council,
R is for Riley, soldier who left Buffy for the Initiative,
S is for Spike, blood-drinking fiend, who saved us all,
T is for Tara, who was taken unwillingly, rest in peace,
U is for Uber Vamps, The First's evil minions,
V is for vengeance, Anya's old gig,
W is for Willow, Buffy's wiccan friend,
X is for Xander, the one who saved the world with his mouth,
Y is for Yellow Crayon, Xander's world-saving speech,
Z is for zoo where many an unexplainable thing did occur.

Becky Churm (14)
Bryngwyn Comprehensive School, Llanelli

Summer Is . . .

Time for fun in the sun,
Rummaging through rock pools,
And buckets filled with warm, golden sand.

When sly seagulls steal ice cream,
While crabbing in a crowded harbour.

Surfing on the white waves,
In the Caribbean.

The scalding sun burns my back.
Slimy jellyfish are washed up on shore.
My toes sink into the sand.

In the street people sweat in smelly shoes,
Others fish in fish-filled lakes
Or explore creepy caves.

That's what summer is!

Megan Barnard (12)
Bryngwyn Comprehensive School, Llanelli

Dogs

Some can be nice, some can be bad,
At the bottom of their paws, they all have pads.
They each have a tail, four paws and a good sense of smell,
They also have soppy noses as well.
They come in all shapes and sizes, and different breeds too,
They chew on anything, even a slipper will do!
They need exercise about twice a day,
But one thing you must not let them do is stray.
A dog will always be your best friend,
But sometimes can drive you round the bend!
All they ask for is food and water,
Some love and care and lots of looking after.
They bark so loudly it can give a fright,
They get scrapes and scratches and can sometimes get into fights!

Kyle Nurse (11)
Bryngwyn Comprehensive School, Llanelli

Rugger's Rugby Poem

R ugby is the game,
U nion is the way,
G ripping the ball,
G reat strides away.
E nergy abounds,
R unning all around,
S crums all together.

R apturous is the crowd,
U nflagging are the players.
G rasping the ball,
B old and proud of them all.
Y ay, hooray for the rugby players.

Every Sunday we play a game,
But who knows who wins?
We bear the conditions of rough or wet
To cheer our winning teams.
We go up the middle and down the side.
They do anything to keep the game alive.
Past the line and what a try!
And, with that, we say goodbye,
Until next Sunday when we hopefully
Score another try!

Elliot Dawe (13)
Bryngwyn Comprehensive School, Llanelli

Rugby

Rugby, rugby, what a game!
Rugby, rugby is the main.
Rugby, rugby is the best,
Well, better than all the rest!

Curtis Morris
Bryngwyn Comprehensive School, Llanelli

My Twin And I

My twin and I are so different, opposite in fact
As I look like him people can't tell us apart
But we like different things, which I soon will reveal
From different hobbies to what we watch on TV.

I like Indian food and Chinese,
He likes steak, chips and peas.

Josh hangs around with people in Years 9 and 8,
I hang around with Year 7, I think they're great.

In PE, Josh likes footie, I prefer rugby where you can get dirty.

Josh likes 'Malcolm In The Middle', the programme on Sky One,
I prefer 'The Simpsons', it's always full of fun.

Josh goes on MSN chatting on the PC
I go out with friends playing mob and footie!

Although us twins might look the same, the difference is immense
We may confuse you but my twin and I are more different from each
other than any one else.

Sam Pomeroy (11)
Bryngwyn Comprehensive School, Llanelli

Summer

S un shining down on my face,
U nder the old trees, sitting for hours on end,
M any endless days of heat shining down from the sun,
M any small insects and animals crawling, slowing under the trees,
E nding the days of longing for heat,
R unning through fields of long green grass.

Sara Grace Griffiths (12)
Bryngwyn Comprehensive School, Llanelli

Cats

Cats big, cats small,
Cats love sleeping anywhere at all.

Cats thin, cats fat,
Cats like tuna and that's that.

Cats naughty, cats nice,
Cats sometimes eat mice.

Cats jump, cats run,
Cats have fun.

Cats black, cats white,
Cats give mice a fright.

Cats pink, cats blue,
I don't think so . . . do you?

Cats silly, cats lazy,
I don't think so, they are crazy.

Samuel Davies (12)
Bryngwyn Comprehensive School, Llanelli

Summer Breeze

The end of May brings a tingle to your nose
People change from jumpers to cool summer clothes
Flowers bloom and the trees go green
The clouds move away so the sun can be seen.

My dog sniffs the air at the smell of charcoaled meat
As barbecues are lit all down the street
The sun goes down as late as nine-thirty
And rises in the morning when the birds are chirpy.

I worship the sun all day
I worship the stars all night
Until the dancing flame of autumn
Turns out the summer light.

Sally Davies (13)
Bryngwyn Comprehensive School, Llanelli

My Mum

In the morning Hedgehog-Head comes into my room,
'Get out of bed!'
She's spiky-haired, she's cuddly too,
and she makes my breakfast,
like mums do.
We pack our bags, then in the car,
I go to school but she goes far.
With blurry fingers she works away,
adding the figures, earning her pay.
Scratchy pens flowing, the work's getting done,
the day soon is over and the evening's begun.
She sits in her armchair, then starts to sew,
flashing needles, glitter and start to glow.
She makes fancy pictures to hang on the wall,
embroidered or crochet, my mum does them all.
And when the day is over and I'm off to bed,
I hug her and kiss her, 'Goodnight Spiky-Head!'

Kimberley Griffiths (11)
Bryngwyn Comprehensive School, Llanelli

My Little Sister

I've got a little sister, she's a pain in the bum,
She's always hanging round me, acting really dumb.
Wherever I go she's bound to follow,
Yelling and screaming like there's no tomorrow.

But when she's good, she's laughing and smiling,
She's like a beautiful flower on a spring morning,
She can be caring, helpful and sweet,
But I really truly love her when she's asleep.

Adam Rees (13)
Bryngwyn Comprehensive School, Llanelli

Me, Myself And I

Teenagers! My mother says
She doesn't understand some of my ways
Music is my passion
I also like the latest fashion

My mother shouts, 'Clean your room!'
I turn my music up *boom, boom, boom*
Cleaning is such a boring job
But if I do it I get a few bob

The spots, the fears and all my tears
Will become a thing of the past
This is all a learning curve
To become a better lass.

Becky Jones (14)
Bryngwyn Comprehensive School, Llanelli

The Creature

The moon was shining bold and bright,
A bloodthirsty howl screeched through the night,
Thick dark fog clouded my way,
I heard heavy footsteps far away,
This beast, this thing was coming closer,
My heart was racing like a roller coaster,
This creature, this monster, was after me,
The fog now thickened till I could not see,
The creature was so close I could here it breathe,
This was a nightmare, I could not leave,
Finally I broke free from the fog,
And saw that this creature was my dog.

Justin Powell (13)
Bryngwyn Comprehensive School, Llanelli

Our World

The world is full of the wrong things,
but we don't know why this is.
People here and there,
throw their garbage everywhere.
The world knows what we're doing,
though we don't have a clue.
All along we sit there not knowing,
what is really going on in our world.
We all wonder sometimes about it,
but just say it's been taken care of.
When we are old and wise,
we'll be sad that we caused this mess that we live in.
Now is the time we should make a start,
before we finish it and all the world comes crashing in on us.
We should take pride in our world,
for it is where we live,
but it shall soon be a big dump site.
A dump site is where we put our rubbish that we cannot keep
though soon the holes that we put our rubbish in
will be filled up everywhere.
Make a start, think about it, don't forget.

Charlotte Beynon
Bryngwyn Comprehensive School, Llanelli

Never

Never give up if you still want to try
Never wipe away tears if you still want to cry
Never say yes when you really mean no
Never say you don't love them if you can't let them go
Because the greatest thing you will ever learn
Is to love and be loved in return.

Hannah Francis (12)
Bryngwyn Comprehensive School, Llanelli

I Love The Beach!

I love the beach
when the sand blows on your face.
I love the beach
when your friends test your pace.
I love the beach
with the water gliding through your toes.
I love the beach
with the dog running with his cold, wet nose.

I love the beach,
playing in paddling pools,
I love the beach,
where there are no schools.
I love the beach!

Joseph Watkeys
Bryngwyn Comprehensive School, Llanelli

The Beautiful Site

Every day and every night
I think and think about this site
A site which is so warm and nice
A site which isn't cold and full of lice
It's in a garden, upon a stream
Where the sun shines like a beam
It's a radiant type of place
It's like an innocent, beautiful face
The grass is no green on the ground
It is so quiet, you can't hear a sound
You can see the glistening in the stream
It's not quite what it seems, it's like a dream.

Aimeé-Francis-Edwards
Bryngwyn Comprehensive School, Llanelli

Holidays

Packing my suitcase, can't wait to go,
It'll be my first time on a plane tomorrow, oh no!
The day is here, I'm ready to go,
Nervous and excited, but happy more.
Arriving at the airport, waiting for my flight,
My mum's face is white, white with fright.
We are on the plane, up in the sky,
There are lots of clouds nearby.
We are about to land in sunny Spain,
I do so hope it doesn't rain.
We've just landed and we're off in the taxi to the hotel,
I'm so tired, I should sleep very well.
I've just woken up to glorious sunshine,
I feel so fine.
I put my swimsuit on and dive in the pool,
At least this way, I'll stay cool.
I'm having the time of my life,
I never want it to end,
But right now I have a lot of postcards to send.

Charlotte Davies (13)
Bryngwyn Comprehensive School, Llanelli

The Dog

T ails wagging, hitting your legs
H air in all shapes and sizes
E ars like velvet, perk up at the sound of their name

D inner time, the leftovers are his
O r maybe, if he's lucky a bone
G ive me a lick to say thanks.

Rebecca Gillman (12)
Bryngwyn Comprehensive School, Llanelli

An Animal's Love

On her soft warm fur,
My tears began to fall,
She came without me asking,
She came without a call.

She comforted me without a sound,
Just her gentle touch,
She knew that I was hurting,
And she knew just how much.

And patiently she waited,
For at least an hour or two,
Until my tears began to fade,
Until there were only a few.

I realised just then,
That an animal's love is true,
They'll always be there by your side,
And they'll never stop loving you.

An animal's love is something kind,
An animal's love that can't speak its mind,
An animal is a pleasure to have around the house,
But isn't quiet as a mouse, *miaow!*

A loving little creature,
So tiny and so small,
That quiet or loud little thing,
That doesn't cry at all.

When she hears you calling,
She sits at the back door,
She waits for you patiently,
And sits on the floor.

Gabrielle Lewis (13)
Bryngwyn Comprehensive School, Llanelli

Be A Hippy!

Riding in a hippy van,
Rave on man!
Peace, love and freedom,
We all need them.

I'm free to be me,
You have war, we make tea,
We have our flower power,
While you have buildings and towers.

How can you buy land,
The grass, trees and sand?
How can you own the sky?
It's not yours to buy.

Be a hippy man,
Ride a hippy van,
Be free,
Happiness is the key.

Laura West (14)
Bryngwyn Comprehensive School, Llanelli

My Dog

My little dog is jet-black,
She likes playing in the back.

She plays on the wall,
Looking for her ball.

She pushes her bowl around the room,
Like you and I would a broom.

She always enjoys eating her food,
Which puts her in a good mood.

My dog and I spend time together,
I know we will be friends forever.

James Lloyd
Bryngwyn Comprehensive School, Llanelli

I've Been A Naughty Girl At School

I've been a naughty girl at school
I wrote a really bad letter.
The person told my teacher in class
And she said I should know better.

I've been a naughty girl at school
I was late for lines outside.
My friends said quick the teacher's coming
So you'd better go and hide.

I've been a naughty girl at school
I pushed somebody in the queue.
They turned right round and pushed me back
And said I really hate you.

I've been a naughty girl at school
I kicked someone in the shin.
They flew right back and tripped right up
And landed head first in the bin.

School is ending, the bell is ringing
We all rushed outside.
I tripped somebody up, their books flew up
And I said, 'I hope you don't mind.'

Stefanie Clark (14)
Bryngwyn Comprehensive School, Llanelli

Can't Write Poems

I can't write poems.
Honestly,
I can't.
Not even a stanza,
Or a single line.
The worst thing of all is making it rhyme.

Lauren Sourbutts (14)
Bryngwyn Comprehensive School, Llanelli

The Stallion

Galloping over the moors he flies
White as snow with crystal eyes
In the despair of blackest night
Freedom wears a man of purest white
His hooves leave no prints, his neigh has no sound
But he seems as real as the stones on the ground
His hair as soft as moonlight's kiss
His form a sight none deserve to miss
He is hope made flesh and brought alive
In his aura hate and fear can never survive
Dawn approaches as night dies
The stallion leaps, flickers, flies
His mane becomes moon, his body the sky
The North Star a single, crystal eye
Death and pain came with the morn
But hope still lives in his pale form
And when daylight severs all its ties
The handsome beast will again rise
Galloping over the moors he flies
White as snow with crystal eyes.

Arianwen Caiach-Taylor (13)
Bryngwyn Comprehensive School, Llanelli

Phenomenon

My life has revolved around this one thing,
The one thing that has kept me going all these years,
The one thing that stopped me breaking down after all the tears,
The one thing that helped me overcome all of my fears.
I let you into my life,
The one thing became obsolete,
You took its place,
If you ever leave, I'll have nothing,
I'll become an empty shell.
You are that one thing.

Molly Jones (14)
Bryngwyn Comprehensive School, Llanelli

Hidden Treasures

I trample through the gritty sand,
With a sieve and shovel in my hand.

I see some building up ahead,
But I turn the other way instead.

I stand on something hard and cold,
It may be treasure, it may be gold.

It could be ancient, it could be new,
Or in the world there could be few.

I start to dig, I'm getting closer,
I may just find a cup and saucer.

But to my amazement all I found,
Was a secret chamber underground.

I saw a lot of steps below,
I thought I better take it slow.

And there inside I found a tomb,
Containing the corpse of Tutankhamun.

I've worked really hard for today,
So please will you now give me my pay.

Natalie Rees (14)
Bryngwyn Comprehensive School, Llanelli

Dance

Dance is such a wonderful thing,
Hip hop to jazz, just shake that thing.
Move along the floor like no one's watching,
You never know, this craze may be catching.
Shake your body and jump to the beat,
Just remember to land on your feet.
Salsa to tap, just like that,
Or dance the samba to a rap.
Just shake your body and move your feet.

Rhian Jones (14)
Bryngwyn Comprehensive School, Llanelli

The World Inside My Head

The final leaf falls to the ground
But no one's there so it makes no sound
Just like me crying in my head
Over everything that has been said.
I may pretend that I can't feel
And that these tears are no big deal.
But in my head where I decide
To keep all my feelings locked up inside
Is a world of hatred, fear and pain
Slowly making me go insane.
As I walk among the people there
Feeling alone, needing them to care
I start wondering how it would be
If I was finally set free.
Is there something in this unfair place
That would leave no tears on my face?
I begin to think this could never be true
That this place is awful through and through.
If I find out that I am right
Then I will give up this fight.
But, until then, I won't admit defeat
I refuse to let my fears and reality meet.

Victoria Griffiths (13)
Bryngwyn Comprehensive School, Llanelli

A Poem On Buffy The Vampire Slayer, The Best TV Show Ever!

B uffy the vampire slayer, one kick arse girl
U ber Vamps got her in a big whirl
F ear and demons never stand in her way
F ighting for the freedom of the world every day
Y ear after year she makes demons pay

T he First Evil tried to destroy us all
H er power made him fall
E ach potential slayer waits for the call

V ampires aren't the only evil she has to face
A lways tries to protect the human race
M aking demons hit the roof
P eople do not know the truth
I n her life she has died twice
R eal life now that would be nice
E vil will pay the price

S pike the vampire with a soul
L oving Buffy and dying for her was his final goal
A ll her life she stayed with her friends
Y ear after year making sure the world never ends
E ven at the end she remained powerful and strong
R emembering that she never went wrong.

Mirella Burgess
Bryngwyn Comprehensive School, Llanelli

School

Why do we have to go to school?
The trouble is there are too many rules.
What to wear, do and say,
Everything has to be a certain way.
Must not run, must not play,
Told to work hard all day.
Teachers seem to always shout,
When I'm bad they send me out.
Stuck in remove when I do wrong,
Stuck there bored all day long.
They tell my mother on the phone,
So I'm in trouble when I get home.
She gives me a row and won't let me out,
All because I messed about.
I wish I was older and had no school,
Every day would be so cool.
Doing what I liked when I can,
Running around with my gang.
I must change my ways mother said,
If I don't I will be dead.
I must learn and do my work,
Or I'll end up a lazy jerk.
To have a great job, I must be good,
And do my work like I should.
If I follow all the rules,
Maybe school could be cool.

David Lewis (13)
Bryngwyn Comprehensive School, Llanelli

Unknown

The meaning of life remains unknown,
Other life, planets and animals remain unknown,
Why does the sea flow?
There are many things unknown.
Are there ghosts?
Are there aliens?
Can time travel be invented?
Are all these tales or stories true?
There is one certain fact,
These things are unknown.

James Thomas
Bryngwyn Comprehensive School, Llanelli

There Was A Boy

There was a boy from Leicester
Who thought he was the bester
At being the biggest pester
But the biggest mistake he had to make
Was pester the big bully Chester.

There was a boy named Dan
Who came to school in a van
Till one day it broke down
And Dan had a big frown
So now he rides on his sister's dog Lester.

There was a boy named Fred
Who was scared of his bed
Because of sleepless nights
The bed gave him frights
So now he sleeps with his father Ted.

Dharmesh Patel (13)
Crown Hills Community College, Leicester

Poem . . .

When you see me in the streets,
You will be thinking, *who is that geek?*
Then you will note, oh it's that freak.
When you see me in the school,
You will be thinking, *what a fool!*
When you see me in the sky,
You will be wondering, *what a fly.*
If you see me in the fight,
You will be wondering, *why is everyone quiet?*
If you see me on a bike,
You will be wondering if there's going to be a fight.
If you see me in a race,
You will be gazing at my nervous face.
If you see me in a crowd,
You will hear everyone shout.
When you see me in the farm,
You will suddenly hear the alarm.
If you know I'm going to the United States,
Then you will see I've made a new mate.

Amardeep Singh (13)
Crown Hills Community College, Leicester

Friendship

If friendship was a stream,
Then ours would be an ocean.
If care was a candle,
Ours would be an open fire,
Burning brightly in the hearth.
If happiness made us jump,
What we share would lift us to the clouds;
And one day, when our time is up,
I pray we can still share our friendship,
In peace.

Veena Patel (13)
Crown Hills Community College, Leicester

The Locked Box

I open the lock
But what will I find?
The voices from my past,
Haunting my mind.

I open the lock,
What have I unleashed?
The pain, the sorrows, the agony,
From day to night I think of him
Seeing only what could be reality.

I open the lock,
What do I see?
The face that was there ten years ago,
The centre of my past,
Which I haven't let go.

I open the lock,
To let it all out,
The secrets which are hidden,
And the pains of my past . . .

Meera Bhanji (14)
Crown Hills Community College, Leicester

Family

I gaze at the starry sky,
As if it holds some secret of mine.
I stare at other families laughing and joking,
And I say, 'I wish they were mine.'
But deep down inside, I know,
This cannot be true,
Because loving families like those,
Are few.

Natalie Doughty (14)
Crown Hills Community College, Leicester

Snow

The snow is falling,
The sky is grey,
We stare out of the window,
Anxious, we want to play.

At last it stops,
But it is cold, we shiver,
Icicles hang like bats,
We poke them, they quiver.

I look at the sky,
Clouds hang overhead,
It is late, I am tired,
I want to go to bed.

The thought of a warm blanket,
And a steaming cup of tea,
Makes me wish that spring was here.
So then I am free!

Suraiya Jagot (13)
Crown Hills Community College, Leicester

The War

The husband goes to war,
Straight out through the front door.
All the family begins to cry,
He knows soon he will see bullets fly,
And he along with many people may also die.
There he is in the trenches,
Along with all the putrid stenches.
Writing letters in his bed,
Hoping that his family is not dead.
Finally the war is over,
The British won the battle at Dover.
The husband returns back from war,
Straight back through the front door.

Tyler Boyce (14)
Crown Hills Community College, Leicester

Family

Family,
There is no such word,
As beautiful as this.

When the nights are cold
And your arms want someone to hold . . .
I call on you.

When the rain is falling,
And I need reassuring . . .
I call on you.

A mother's loving arms and a father's guidance,
A brother or sister may hide in silence
Until a later date
As we grow up we come closer.

Although we may be far apart,
Taking on our own lives
Along life's family path
With our own sons and daughters . . .
They call on us!

Carrie-Ann Bugby (13)
Crown Hills Community College, Leicester

I Saw The Sky

It darkened as the sun went down,
The sky turned grey to black.
The darkness affected the people and the animals.
The people settled to sleep
As the darkness fell into the sky.
The animals,
Some slept in a slumber
And others woke to stalk their prey.
Then soon the darkness cleared,
The sun rose to start a new day.

Nilesh Odedra (13)
Crown Hills Community College, Leicester

The FA Cup Final

Eleven football players on each side walk on the pitch,
The whistle blows and a midfielder has a stitch,
Eighty-eight minutes' play and the ball is in the back of the net,
We need to get a shot on target.
In the last minute we scored,
The crowd applaud.
It's one-all and the fans cheer and shout,
This match sent us to a penalty shoot-out.
They scored four,
We scored five,
The goalkeeper must save this goal . . .
For us to feel happy and not cold.
The shot is taken and the ball goes wide,
We won the game, we almost cried.
We stood up tall with our hands raised up,
We have won the FA Cup!

Ali Madarbukus (14)
Crown Hills Community College, Leicester

The Aching Heart

I let you break my heart once,
I let you break it twice.
I thought you loved me,
Oh! How I was wrong.
You're just another typical guy.
I wasted all my time thinking about you.
You let me think you loved me,
You let me think you cared.
So, now you've moved on,
Without so much as a backward glance,
And it's goodbye forever.
So why don't you break my heart,
Just one more time,
Just for good luck.

Kerry Byrnes (14)
Crown Hills Community College, Leicester

Slavery Poem

We come to a new country in a ship,
We are stuck together so tight,
We can't even move our lips.

Our own race, our own people, deceive us
So many people parting from their loved ones,
They make so much fuss.

New country we come, but with grief,
Meeting new people who don't look like us,
Is much more grief.

Every day and every night, sweeping and dusting,
Washing and cleaning, clearing and dying.
This is what we call slavery!
Do you?

Hardik Purohit (14)
Crown Hills Community College, Leicester

A Year Away From Me

I know it's only one year
That you will be away
But it feels far more than that
Each long and lonely day.

A day without a friend is like
A city turned to sand,
A garden turned to dust,
An ocean far from land.

Time enters a slow motion zone,
Repeating endlessly.
A tearful hole in my heart,
Till you return to me.

Ashish Raja (13)
Crown Hills Community College, Leicester

I Am . . .

I am a fairy
I can do a lot of magic
I am very wary
I can also make things very tragic.

I am a flower
I can open very wide
I am as high as a tower
I can live inside and outside.

I am a fish
I can swim very fast
I am living in a dish
I can swim and never be last in a race.

I am a frog
I can jump very high
I am good in the fog
I can be very shy.

Laura Muir (13)
Kilsyth Academy, Kilsyth

Eilidh Smith

She is orange, bright and outgoing
She is like 7.30 at night
When the fun begins.
She is sunny like a summer's day,
She is fun like a trampoline.
She is fun and casual
Like a pair of flip-flops.

Caroline Hood (11)
Kilsyth Academy, Kilsyth

My Friend Eilidh

She is light yellow,
As bright as the sun.

She is 3.35,
Always up for some fun!

She is happy, like spring,
As fresh as a daisy.

She is like ice cream,
Always parties like crazy!

She is a trampoline,
Funny and jumpy!

She is cool, casual jeans,
And always looks funky.

Katy McGlinchey
Kilsyth Academy, Kilsyth

My Friend

She is girly pink, flirting for fun.
She is funny and sweet, as bright as the sun.
She is a 4.30 person, can't wait to get out.
She is always smiling, you will never see a pout.

She is like a diamond ring, sparkling with joy,
She is like a trampoline, always jumping like a toy.
She always dresses casually, always goes with the crowd.
She isn't always quiet, she loves to be loud.

Amy Woods
Kilsyth Academy, Kilsyth

Alyson

She is baby-blue, cool and casual
And full of exciting fun.

She is a nice hot day in the summer,
Happy in the sun.

She is 3.35, running from school,
She can't wait to get home.

She is pizza and chips with tomato sauce,
Never eating alone.

She is a big and bouncy trampoline,
Giggling all the time.

She is a pair of flip-flops in the summer,
Wearing colours red, pink and lime!

Rachel McGale (12)
Kilsyth Academy, Kilsyth

Kelsey

She is pyjamas, warm and soft.
She is 3.35, freedom at last.
She is fun and funky pizza, up for a laugh.
She is a stormy November night.
She is an artist's palette, green, blue and white.

Shelly Bamford (12)
Kilsyth Academy, Kilsyth

Shelly

Shelly's like a tie-dye towel,
That stands out on the beach.
Whatever mood she feels like,
They're always within reach.

She is like at 9pm,
When the parties really start,
When everyone is having fun,
And everyone looks the part.

She is like a lightning storm,
On a bright summer's day.
She may not be what you expect,
She'll surprise you in some way!

She is like a cheeky Smartie,
That has just rolled away.
How can you scold a Smartie?
She'll get off with murder one day!

She is like a mobile phone,
Because she's always there.
It doesn't matter where she is,
She sounds off without a care.

She is like a flip-flop,
Impractical when it's muddy,
Impractical nearly any day,
But, hey! She's my best buddy!

Hannah Boyce (12)
Kilsyth Academy, Kilsyth

My Best Friend

She is a bursting bright green,
She is a rainy day, always in some muddles.
She is a girl who likes to stay
Up late on school nights.
And she loves eating ice cream,
She is a fluffy cushion giving me cuddles,
She is rainbow-coloured stripy tights
And is my best friend, Kate.

Emily Morrison
Kilsyth Academy, Kilsyth

My Best Friend Emily!

She is like a colourful rainbow
She is 12 noon on a happy day
She is like the sunny weather
She is like cream cakes and honey
She is like a comfy sofa made of leather
She is like a comfy pair of slippers.

Stacey McMahon
Kilsyth Academy, Kilsyth

My Pal Jack

He is the colour yellow, because he is usually happy.
He is 1.30 on a Saturday afternoon.
He is a whirlwind, because he is mental.
He is a ghetto blaster, because he's really loud.
He is a Thistle jersey, standing out in the crowd.

Daniel Muir
Kilsyth Academy, Kilsyth

If Scientists Didn't Have Brains

Scientists are everywhere in the world,
Or how would we be able to have our hair curled?

There would be no cars or trains,
Simply if scientists didn't have the brains.

Who would make up inventions?
Not teachers, they only give detentions.

If there weren't scientists, we would be living in the Stone Age,
But now everything you need to know is in a book on a page.

If scientists weren't coming up with new ideas,
Everyone would have to face up to their fears.

But the good thing is, scientists are there,
And they do everything, because they enjoy it and they care.

Albert Einstein is the most famous scientist ever,
No one can beat him, never.

Amy Stewart (12)
Kilsyth Academy, Kilsyth

Victoria Marshall

She's like one in the afternoon,
When we meet for fun.

She's like baby-pink,
Cute and cuddly.

She's like chocolate,
Sweet and sugary.

She's like an easy chair,
Strong and comfortable.

She's like a pair of pyjamas,
Warm and cosy.

She's like the sun,
Warm and bright.

Marie Quinn (12)
Kilsyth Academy, Kilsyth

Sparks

Great minds think alike in lots of wonderful ways,
We don't know what sets it off, but we always give our praise.

Sparks, sparks, all in their heads,
Sparks, sparks, well, dreaming in bed,
Sparks, sparks, all year long,
Sparks, sparks, they're never gone.

Many great inventions come from these special ones,
With hard work, determination, as well as having fun.

Sparks, sparks, all in their heads,
Sparks, sparks, well, dreaming in bed,
Sparks, sparks, all year long,
Sparks, sparks, they're never gone.

We benefitted from crazy ideas, like transport, high in the sky,
Or magical rides that go really fast and roller coasters way up high.

Sparks, sparks, all in their heads,
Sparks, sparks, well, dreaming in bed.
Sparks, sparks, all year long,
Sparks, sparks, they're never gone.

Wherever we are, whatever we do,
These minds will be where we like,
Always there for us when we need them most . . .
For after all great minds think alike.

Samantha Croal (12)
Kilsyth Academy, Kilsyth

Elephants Can't Dance

Elephants have big enormous feet,
But when they walk it's like a beat.
They thump and bang and wallop and crash
But does that mean that they can't dance?

Elephants have big enormous ears,
A mouse is an elephant's biggest fear.
An elephant can't fly or prance,
But does that mean that they can't dance?

Elephants have delicate tails,
But if it was weighed it'd break the scales.
Elephants are careful not to stand on ants,
But does that mean that they can't dance?

Elephants have big, round bellies,
Their feet can't even fit into wellies.
Elephants are heavier when they come from France,
But does that mean that they can't dance?

Victoria Marshall
Kilsyth Academy, Kilsyth

Kilsyth

K ilsyth is cool
I t has a great swimming pool
L ots of nice people
S pires and a steeple
Y ou may even note it
T hat Kilsyth Rangers are getting promoted
H ail thou Kilsyth.

Callum Holmes (13)
Kilsyth Academy, Kilsyth

A Walk In The Rainforest

I hear leaves rustling through the breezy wind,
I turn round - 'What's that?' I ask.
Water rushing down narrow hills, making waterfalls,
The sound's amazing!
Butterflies fluttering in their families, blue, red and purple
They seem happy to have wings.

I see bromeliads big and bright waiting for something to catch.
Frogs pouncing about, croaking madly as they hop merrily.
Plants with gigantic leaves, some over a metre,
And bigger than me.

I smell the relaxing lavender, casting me to sleep
As it drifts through the air,
As that happens it makes me feel at home.
The Earth's richness feels so refreshing.

I touch long ferns, reaching high above,
Higher and higher they go.
Massive trees up in the sunlight
With lianas twirling down and down.
Twigs snapping as I crunch the ground
They feel rough and smooth.

I taste sweetness from the peaceful vanilla and mint
So strong it takes my breath away.
Herbs dancing in bundles, swaying side to side.
Fruit with its citrus tastes, juicy and sweet.

I feel relaxed as the water runs deep into the gorges,
When the sun sets through the trees,
Listening to the creatures singing their tunes,
Excited, imagining what I'm going to find.
Maybe a new animal or a medicine or food.
I just can't wait to explore.
Heartbroken that so many species and other things
Are going to die because of us.
Cutting it down for money, paper, gold and furniture.
I'm astonished
That if we didn't have rainforests we wouldn't be
Alive!

Carrie Jasmine Kaur Lota (12)
Kilsyth Academy, Kilsyth

A Rainy Day

It's raining today
The sky is black
No sunshine today
It might come back . . .

The trees are all wet
And very green.
The burns are all full
Like a great big stream.

A streak of lightning
To light the sky.
A blast of thunder,
Very nearby.

At last the sunshine starts to peep through,
Goodbye rainy day,
Goodbye to you.

Matthew Thomson (12)
Kilsyth Academy, Kilsyth

My Sister

My sister is the best,
Even though she thinks of me as a pest,
But I couldn't love her less!

My sister has a fab mind,
And she is so clever and kind,
But I couldn't love her less!

My sister is so great,
Even though she's always late,
But I couldn't love her less!

My sister is out of this world,
But I couldn't love her less!

Gemma Butterly (12)
Kilsyth Academy, Kilsyth

My Dog Clyde

My dog Clyde is just so cool,
But, like most dogs, a bit of a fool.
He likes to play with the dog next door,
The only dog he doesn't want to floor.
Saying this, he isn't bad,
But say it to him and he'll go mad.

He's gold and white, he's so cute,
But don't be fooled if you're a newt.
He'll eat you alive and you'll soon be dead,
So when Clyde is around, go back to bed.

Clyde's tail is long and bushy,
I really think that he'd like sushi.
When we went to the sea, he dived straight in,
And chased the fish till he couldn't swim.

So at this point Clyde is calm,
As I am throwing him bits of ham.
But even if Clyde sounds nuts,
I love my dog Clyde to bits and bits.

Andrew Fowler (14)
Kilsyth Academy, Kilsyth

Rain

When it rains,
It forgets to go away.
It pours down
And floods the drains.
People get soaked
And start to moan,
'Go away rain,
And leave us alone!'

Jamie Turner (12)
Kilsyth Academy, Kilsyth

Experiment Gone Wrong!

'The outcome will be brilliant,' I said to myself,
As I took Mum's Chanel No 5 down from the shelf.
It lay in the wrapper, tied up plain and neat,
I unscrewed the bottle and the air grew sweet.
Mum had shouted and filled me with fear,
She couldn't care less when my eyes shed a tear.

I looked around the bathroom,
Picked up two bottles of *K-9 perfect pooch* shampoo,
A tube of toothpaste, some shower gel,
Mixed together and time would tell.
I grinned with pleasure, my deed was done,
I never knew evil could be so much fun.
The cap went back on and I screwed it strong,
There was no going back, was I right or wrong?

I shook the glass bottle right there and then,
All of this happened when I was ten,
I played the game, I got the blame,
I did the crime and now the time.

Rebecca Fitzsimmons (12)
Kilsyth Academy, Kilsyth

Emma Lou

My name is Emma Lou
I am the very best.
If you don't believe me
Then put me to the test.

I am a whiz at maths skills,
And aced the English test.
Now that I have proved myself,
You know I am the bet!

Emma Gray
Kilsyth Academy, Kilsyth

Premiership

P owerful shots bulge the back of the net!

R eferee waves away appeals for a penalty!

E lectric atmosphere amongst the fans!

M anagers pacing the touchline, fuming in outrage!

I mmense tricksters showing off skills in front of the crowd!

E xhausted midfielders run the length of the field!

R ifled shots curling away from the keeper into the corner!

S kilful step-overs, puzzle defenders!

H orrendous mistake by the keeper gives the striker a goal!

I njury to star player, worried, trembling manager

P remiership, the ultimate league!

Tom Hunt (11)
Lockyer's Middle School, Wimborne

Cheesy

Stirring from the depths of
The evil, cheesy lair.
Where no light did enter,
Not even a sliver;
Lay this small, hairy thing,
Which smelt of mouldy socks,
With the colour of blue
And red and green small spots.
It lay there in the dark,
Just waiting for some day
When it could come out and
Release its mighty stench.

Sharnie Mead (12)
Lockyer's Middle School, Wimborne

The True Story Of Goldilocks

Goldilocks was in the forest
With her boyfriend Mr Norridge.
While in the cottage in the wood,
The three bears ate up all their pud.
Goldilocks was far too late
She thought it was a different date.
The three bears ate their yummy porridge
While Goldilocks kissed Mr Norridge.
The three bears went out for a walk
And Goldilocks began to talk.
'That little cottage over there,
I'm almost sure they'll do my hair.'
But just as they walked through the gate,
There they met an awful fate.
Mr Bear said, 'Goldilocks,
You're late, did you catch chickenpox?
We'll have extra in our porridge,
Tomorrow we'll have Mr Norridge!'
And with that he grabbed the man,
And home to Mummy, Goldi ran.
I need not say much more than that
But three bears got rather fat!

Katherine Williams (11)
Lockyer's Middle School, Wimborne

Shrek

Shrek lives in a swamp with nothing around,
Except for the odd tree planted in the ground.
One day he meets a donkey with a very large mouth,
So they go on a quest to Farquar's place which is south.

Farquar wanted Fiona the princess,
The ginger one, wearing a green dress.
He wanted someone to find her instead of him,
Because he knew the castle was grim.

Shrek and Donkey won the fight,
They went to find Fiona without any fright.
So Shrek and Donkey went straight away,
Well they couldn't go to the swamp where they couldn't stay.

Not much happened on the way,
Apart from Donkey having a lot to say.
They got to the castle with a load of fright
But when Shrek rescued Fiona, they were full of delight.

When they got back to their place,
Fiona had a different face.
So in the end, Shrek married her,
And they all lived happily ever after.

Thomas Joy (12)
Lockyer's Middle School, Wimborne

The Tortoise And The Hare

Here is one of Aesop's fables
Very interesting and plenty able
To grab your attention fair and square
For it is about a tortoise and hare.
The hare, one day, declared a race,
For his running was completely ace.
The tortoise, he did agree,
Though everyone knew who the winner would be.
At the start line the hedgehog said, 'Go!'
They were off but *whoa!*
The hare was off at such a pace,
Poor tortoise was left at the beginning of the race.
A little further along the track,
The hare stopped for a tasty snack.
The tortoise finally caught up,
And rolling on the floor was an empty wine cup!
The bewildered tortoise looked around
And saw the hare sleeping soundly on the ground.
However, he carried on with little fright,
For the finish line was now in sight.
The hare woke up to wild clapping,
And so ran off without much chatting.
But, alas, the tortoise had already won,
And the hare's anger had just begun!

Jennifer Bolton (11)
Lockyer's Middle School, Wimborne

Cinderella

Listen carefully and listen well,
For I have a story to tell,
About a girl, lovely and kind,
The kindest girl you could ever find.

She had some sisters, there were two,
Who were very ugly and looked like poo.
They treated her like a piece of dirt,
So she could never ever flirt.

Oh and don't forget the evil stepmum,
Who didn't even allow her to hum.
So when the invitation came,
Cindy couldn't go again.

Cindy was locked up in a tower,
So all she did was look at the flowers.
So then the fairy godmother came,
And changed Cindy's rags which were very lame.

So then Cindy rushed to the ball,
In a gown and a very big shawl.
She had a dance with the prince,
Then it struck 12 and Cindy flinched.

'Oh, I must get back to my home.'
She rushed down the stairs as she was thrown.
She realised one of her shoes was missing,
But ran on, cursing and dissing.

The prince looked and looked for his pearl,
The stepmum didn't know Cindy was his girl.
Cindy then tried on the shoe,
The prince knew that she was his clue.
Then they were to be carried
Off to the place where they got married.

Amy Prewer (12)
Lockyer's Middle School, Wimborne

Loch Ness Monster

In the depths and darkness
Of a stirring, horror lake,
Named the Scottish Loch Ness
Not asleep but wide awake,
Lives a lonely, starving creature
Only eating meat with its giant jaw
With hundreds of other terrible features
Such as its sharp, cutting claws.
Its dark and gloomy lair
Fills any heart with fear.

Heidi Beasley (11)
Lockyer's Middle School, Wimborne

My Ballad

I had a dream
Not nice, but mean.
Knives were around,
But no one to be found.

But then again, I heard a scream
Coming from my dear Celine.
I heard a shout, what did it mean?
The death of her, my sweet, dear queen.

My dear queen was lying there,
Lying there with no one's care.
All they could do was stand and stare
Or was this murder an awful dare.

My friend Samantha had a dream,
She was at the cinema screen.
I was about to rush down to the rescue
But first I had to nip down to Tesco.

Brandon Hulme (12)
Longton High School, Stoke-on-Trent

Mornings

Every time I wake up
My body feels hollow.
My throat's so dry I can't swallow
I dread waking up.

Every time I wake up,
I wish I didn't have to
I detest waking up to that crew
I dread waking up.

Every time I wake up
My whole body shivers.
I cry, my tears make rivers
I dread waking up.

Every time I wake up
I look back on my life.
My life is strife
I dread waking up.

Abi Shubotham (13)
Longton High School, Stoke-on-Trent

Untitled

School is very boring
I hate getting up in the morning
But if I don't move my mum starts roaring,
'Get up or you'll be late this morning!'
But I say, 'Who cares, because school is boring!'

Natasha Harper & Louise Shaw (13)
Longton High School, Stoke-on-Trent

Untitled

I hate school,
School hates me.
It's really boring,
I just can't see
Why kids aren't snoring.

There was a man called Bill
Who liked to write with a quill.
One day he fell
Straight down the well
Now he is stuck on the pill.

Footie is good,
Rolling in the mud.
Making you dirty
Like Mr Berty.

The goals I score,
Make me want more.
I know I can,
With support from my fans.

I play as a striker,
My boots are Nike
I like footie so much
I would give anything to clutch
The World Cup!

Grant Cork (12)
Longton High School, Stoke-on-Trent

England

I am an England fan,
We always have a plan.
And when it's going wrong,
We have to sing a song.

In 1966 they made us proud
Because we had won a very special crown.
And if it is going wrong
We still support till the 90 minutes have gone.

And when we beat Germany 5-1
It was the best that we'd ever won.
We should have won 6-1
But we didn't because the referee's
Wig fell off and never went back on.

Nathan Wilkinson
Longton High School, Stoke-on-Trent

Summer

S hining sun so bright and so warm.
U mbrellas are gone till autumn returns.
M elting chocolate and melting ice cream,
M any more summers to come with warmth.
E nergy of the sun will start to die out
R ain comes and we say goodbye to the sun,
    until it returns in 12 months time.

Nicola Johnson (12)
Longton High School, Stoke-on-Trent

Magical Places

Running rivers on the mountain glade,
Sitting happily in the shade.
We rest our toes in the water below,
It's really quiet here you know.
We'll have some lunch and a glass of wine
We don't care about the time.
We sit and wonder about things gone by
As we watch the moving, magical sky.
We see the ripples in the pools below
And the reflection of the bright rainbow.
There's so much beauty all around,
This magical place that we're glad we've found.

Natalie Dudley (13)
Longton High School, Stoke-on-Trent

My Poems

There was a girl called Elle,
With a widescreen telly.
She watched it all day,
On the sofa she lay
And ate all her mother's jelly.

Hannah was in a race,
She went at a very fast pace.
She won the cup,
And she was made up
And she danced around the field.

Jade Tinsley (13)
Longton High School, Stoke-on-Trent

Football Stadium

I walked in a stadium full of smoke,
I went to the bar to get some Coke.
I saw two men having a fight
And one of the men hit the other with all his might.

I went to check if he was all right
And he looked such a sight.
And then he started to cry
And let out a really big sigh.

We went to the stands and saw it was sunny
When they kicked off it was kind of funny.
One of the players fell down on his bum
And acted like he had been shot by a gun.

Lee Lovatt & Aaron Phillips (11)
Longton High School, Stoke-on-Trent

Cars

Cars can be quick,
Cars can be slow,
What is next?
We just don't know.

There are millions all over the world,
There are types galore,
But soon there will be more.

I love all cars,
There's two or three,
I wonder what the next will be!

Ben Dyke (13)
Longton High School, Stoke-on-Trent

My Mum

My mum is a top mum,
She helps me all the time.
She's like my best friend
Because I see her all the time.
I can't live without her,
She means so much to me,
I hope she never leaves.

Rachael Lindop (13)
Longton High School, Stoke-on-Trent

Untitled

There is a boy called John,
Who is a big con.
He does whatever it takes,
To sell people fakes.
Most of the time he sells them on.

Craig Grestow (12)
Longton High School, Stoke-on-Trent

Dancing Queen

Friday night I go dancing,
It sets my heart prancing.
I look so fine,
All the boys are mine.
I'm the one they're fancying.

Danielle Minor & Amelia Wiggins (12)
Longton High School, Stoke-on-Trent

Murder

Cold, dark, deep into the night
Not one person was in sight.
All of a sudden down came the rain,
Then I heard a voice from the lane.

Then I stopped and listened carefully,
All of a sudden I heard footsteps gently.
Then I jumped and hid behind the ice cream van
And then I looked, there was a man.
The man was not standing up,
He was lying on the ground drenched in blood.

Kainat Rehmin
Longton High School, Stoke-on-Trent

Ali G

The king of bling
Demands respect
Diss his posse
And you'll get decked.

They wear their yellow gear
Showing Westside as the best
Big up the Eastside
And they won't be impressed.

Remember the name Ali G
He demands RESTECP.

Heena Hussain (13)
Longton High School, Stoke-on-Trent

Can Anyone See?

Can anyone see what I can see?
A world of myriad dreams exist
Revolving round an eternity
Of fleeting thoughts and dappled mists.
Humanity's paths weave a tapestry
And each man has his turns and twists.

Dukes and duchesses,
Monarchs and earls,
All in fine dresses,
Wigs, coats and curls
Dining on suppers
Of red wine and pearls

While downtrodden workers
With nothing to eat,
No shirt on their backs and
No shoes on their feet
Go home to dank dwellings
And quietly weep.

Yet what the eye doesn't see
The mind doesn't ponder
So through refuge camps
And slums take a wander
For those faces may not be
Around for much longer.

Can anyone see what I can see?
Limitless possibilities for good are here
But our world is split by disunity,
We choose prejudice, greed and fear.
We strive for gold in dappled mists
Feeding off hatred and vengeful tears
Creating scars that take centuries to heal,

Instead of years.

Josh Holt (18)
Michael Hall School, Forest Row

Moonlight

Suicide by moonlight

Silently sliding on silvery space,
Slicing its placid skin is a canoe.
Quietly plashes a paddle with grace,
Radiating flames of moon in the lagoon.
In the centre moonlight hovers by you,
Watching your mind calculate its recession.
Gleaming in the night a knife slices you,
Water fusing blood, pools of expression.
Below the surface a human still dies.
Moonlight in shallows smothers with a ray.
A body sunken in depression lies,
Lost in fissures of light, solidly grey.
 In sleep the body can rest in the deep.
 In slumber the mind can quietly weep.

Mind by moonlight

Silently gliding on a pure surface,
Slicing freezing cold lips is a canoe.
Quiet is the paddle that propels grace,
Radiating flames of moon on the lagoon.
In the centre the moon's in expectation,
Watching your mind dancing, struggling with life.
Glowing in the blackness, a reflection,
Golden in the blinding radiance of life.
Below the surface a fear of death dies.
Moonlight calming the shallow with a ray.
A mind sunken in depression rises,
Floating over fissures of light subtly.
 Above shallows the mind shining can love.
 Without fear, the soul can fly like a dove.

Alexander Willink
Michael Hall School, Forest Row

Grown-Ups

I remember when I was a little girl
And still gazing up at the world in awe
And my mother would tell me, 'No.
You can do as you please when you grow up,' she'd scold.
The silent question remained unasked in my impressionable mind
For fear of exposing my ignorance:
Are grown-ups perfect then?

For years I longed to be older,
Thinking of growing into adulthood
As an ascent to infallibility
Grown-up, always seemed so far in the distance
Because I felt I still had so much to learn
How could I be grown up when I did not yet know everything?
It was only when talking to an old woman
Who seemed oblivious to the ways of the world
That I came to a conclusion:
Being a grown-up has nothing to do with age.
We are children, wondering when we will become perfect
Wondering when we will become grown-ups.

Then what makes us grown-up? Wisdom? Knowledge?
Some insight to which we children are none the wiser?
Is it when you can do as you please? No.
The truth is there is no *do as you please in this life*
Just *do what you could not before*
And the things you could do before, you can no longer do.
So then what? I propose that there is no better, but stages
So when Mummy told me, 'You can do as you please when
                                        you grow up'.
I wish I had been grown-up enough to say, 'Are grown-ups perfect?'

Sara Doron (17)
Michael Hall School, Forest Row

Patterns

Silently walking, flicking through
Newspapers, memories of a long-lost dream.

Walking with no direction
Aimlessly trying to read,
With the up, down, up, down of every step.

Flicking between ideas, thoughts
And feelings, mentioning to myself
The wisps of wind that flicker like flames
Across the immense dimensions of the mind.

Through a desert of brightly coloured pictures
Imitating that of a secret dream
Lost in the backward abysm of time
Amongst sweet, sweet flowers.

Newspapers comment on the ideals of children
By mentioning the harmful pain that a world of adults live in
Creating for me, pictures in my mind,
Pictures that reflect death.

Memories are sweet, sweet flowers
That come in the up, down, up down of every step
That walk inwardly in time with an hourglass
Through pictures of bright colours, black and white
Imitating life and death; that are memories of a long-lost dream.

Maddy Worsley (18)
Michael Hall School, Forest Row

Freedom

Our land has been taken; we are all but free,
Africa has been divided to many a colony.
Our lives have been ruined, some were made into slaves,
Our work is dangerous, yet we try to be brave.
Our culture, religion and more have been taken,
We have been split into tribes beyond our tradition.
We've been given protection and some education
Our fellow black brothers now govern the south,
Some of our debts we hear maybe forgiven,
While we now have new medicines to put in our mouths
And modern technology which now we've been given,
So life's not so hopeless, whatever you think.

Why do we have to be slaves in our haven?
We want to be free and live our own lives.
Some disagree with the things we've been given,
Want nothing to do with new methods or drives.
Our country is beautiful, that's what we love,
We'd rather just grow with no outside shove.

Vanessa Odell (15)
Michael Hall School, Forest Row

The Dance

Grey, bulbous clouds, swollen and pale hang above
In a bleached sky, cut by buildings arranged
At right angles reaching upwards in a strange
Desperate plea; while the people push and shove
And scuttle in some crazy dance of
Patchwork colours that disintegrate, change
Outward and around me, beyond the range
Of my vision, like the buildings above.
I'm alone and I turn inward to my
Own damp thoughts; echoing the people who
Twist by me, anonymous in their cry
Although they share the breath of London through
I trudge on and am lost to the bleached sky
And the trudging of people all lost too.

Merle Hunt
Michael Hall School, Forest Row

Africa

They came as if from nowhere,
Our sacred earth they take,
They accuse us of sins and treachery,
And our families they break.

They tell us that we know nothing,
About culture and how life goes,
They may have advanced education,
But how little they do know.

We've walked this earth for centuries,
We've learnt how to care for its crop,
But they're spreading like plague over this soil,
It's too late now, it won't stop.

No longer do I walk freely,
Across my native land,
I'm enslaved to work from dawn 'til dusk,
With cut and blood-drenched hands.

My children are crying and starving,
And you tell us this is help,
If we'd taken everything that you had,
How do you think you would have felt?

You destroyed a way of life,
You took freedom and tore it apart,
You may be trying to fix our world,
But you cannot mend our hearts.

Beth Pridham (15)
Michael Hall School, Forest Row

Rebirth

How can I begin to describe the might
Of spring's first blossoms as nature unfurls
The glorious dawn of awakened light
Or the glistening dewdrops, morning pearls?
How can I ever define the pure grace
Of the curve of a swift's wing when in flight
Or gaze upon all mankind's youthful face
As reflected in the uplifting sight
Of colour born, tinting Earth's grey canvas?
Soon to be bright, gilded in regal tones
Echoes chorus of hope at morning mass
The sound, through lonely hills and hearts it roams.
How can I begin to describe the might
Of God's creation, the rebirth of life?

Rhiannon Lake-Edwards (16)
Michael Hall School, Forest Row

Fusion

Rush, the breathing wind brushes silky green
Stalks that quiver and sweet pink, peeping through
Befriends flowering stars that bob and dream.
The dancing bees rest on velvety-blue
Petals, hinted beyond the grass and trees.
Nature's choir, the birds, lift the heart flying
Weaves with the musky scent wends on the breeze.
All the world is still and nature is sighing.
Would that all life be as beautiful, clear.
Then all dreams could soar like birds in the air
And nature's heart would beat so all could hear.
Her pale arms would reach, touch that which is fair,
Eyes glisten brightly, her hair fresh and wild
And we should respect her, we are her child.

Abra Hunt
Michael Hall School, Forest Row

Postcard From Paradise

I dreamed the other night that you came back,
Tried so hard to follow, but you were gone,
Awoke alone; prisoner of the black
Of my empty room, just me on my own.
So many tears make my mascara bleed,
Leaving stains on my face; they say,
You're someone I was intended to need,
And for your absence, my own mind must pay.
Are you gone? Or are you just out of sight?
They told me Heaven was a holiday,
But if it really is, why don't you write
Like wish you were here? It's not much to say.
It's hurting so badly; I'm missing you.
I often wonder, do you miss me too?

Stephanie Kerridge (16)
Michael Hall School, Forest Row

Caught In Time

Ha-ha! This letter bears a royal mark,
But the contents can only contain pain.
Alone outside the dog, so free to bark,
Inside, my heart drops a beat with the strain.
She was so free and beautiful at heart
Like cubs playing around their mother's chest;
But to a surgeon's bed she must depart
'Til death do rest his head upon her breast.
I place a lily into her hand;
The lily, like her, cut off at its prime;
A tear rolls off my cheek and hits the sand
On the beach I walk alone, caught in time.
This one beach is the symbol of our love.
My darling, don't ever forget my love.

Euan Crowder (16)
Michael Hall School, Forest Row

Untitled

When I am left to muse and to ponder
Shadows of past times awake in my mind
I crave back the time, wasted in wonder
Searching for hopeful dreams never made mine.
Then I sigh a fresh grief and shed a tear
For all who I have lost along the way
Whose paths have strayed from mine I fear
Leaving me alone to face darker days.
What deeds have made me so worthy to live,
When misfortune should come to such good saints?
I can't help wondering what I'm meant to give,
If failure seems to haunt my every move,
But whilst I ponder on what could have been,
All sorrow is lost and new dreams made clean.

Ben Holt (16)
Michael Hall School, Forest Row

What Is Love?

What is love?
Is love a good thing or a bad?
Emotion, devotion, the repetitive thunders of a heartbeat forced into a
tunnel of excitement and fear.
For love is anything but clear.
How can a person be in love one minute and the next use it as a
curtain, shutting out the light?
When God invented love, how did he describe and build such a thing?
How can anyone describe love?
Only once you have experienced love can you begin to feel the
happiness, but sometimes grief.
Love is like the world; each country so different that you can only begin
to experience the wonders and disappointments, once you have
visited them.

Sapphire Allard (15)
Michael Hall School, Forest Row

Clouds

I have witnessed many wonderful days
And I have felt many happy feelings;
But today, the thick clouds of my heavy
Emotions mask him from me yet again.
When we are next together will be when
The clouds part and my sunny emotions
Shine out. 'Til then, anger overrides this
And dense, black clouds cast shadows among us.
This distance between us becomes greater,
As the black sky becomes more overcast.
A moment of utter stillness passes.
Then suddenly streams of sunlight shine down
Upon my mask of gloomy emotions,
Ultimately, unveiling the true me.

Holly Westlake (16)
Michael Hall School, Forest Row

Fallen Love

What is romance, but a take on love?
And the feeling of the falling dove,
The memories left lying on the cobbled ground
With the everlasting petal that's found.
The care of the feeling that gives it there,
And the magical image left there to stare,
Which bubbles inside me, to an angry glare.
The water that lies on the eye below
The shadow reflects from the golden sun
The clouds from above and love which is led
From the ever-reforming line of thread.
What this means is nothing to me . . .
But the take on love,
Which is stolen from the dying dove.

Jessica Bleach (16)
Michael Hall School, Forest Row

Untitled

Trapped, caught,
Living in my own time.
Though I am here,
I am also there,
Wandering between two worlds,
My own world,
Or the real world?

I like my world,
All is good,
But soon I step
Into a different place,
With death, destruction,
Abuse of other race,
No one is content,
Greed has taken over,
Always wanting more
And never quite knowing,
What is waiting at your door.
Good news,
Bad news,
A newborn child?
An old man, mild,
Has passed away,
Before the first light of day,
Lonely in his jail cell,
Now he rests his head,
Upon his cold bed,
A final resting place,
The world, such a disgrace,
With no familiar face,
No one to miss him,
He is gone,
Fate has abandoned him,
In a cruel, terrible world.

Soon I will be back in my own world
And a shot of guilt hits my heart,
Sharp as a knife,
Knowing what I've left behind,
Leaving that old man to die,
To the world he saw,
We turn a blind eye.
Drifting into an eternal dream,
Full of sadness,
Of days gone by,
Of childhood torment,
Playing mind games,
Telling lies,
Could you imagine,
The pain of that old man,
Regretting everything,
He ever did?
Never telling,
Of when he was a child,
Of all his pain,
Suffering, heartache,
But regretting more,
What he didn't do.
About not telling his sweetheart,
How he loved her.
About not telling,
Me or you,
How much he hated this selfish world,
Full of hate
And ice-cold stares.
That is all he saw
And felt the consequences,
Of an unjust law.
Shouts were all he heard,
Not the sweetest singing,
Of the morning bird.

I think I would prefer my world,
But it was just a dream,
Only a dream.

Louisa Taplin (13)
Priory School

What Is A Great Mind?

Is a great mind a scientist,
A physicist like Einstein or Newton,
A biologist like Darwin, or
A chemist like Dalton?

Is a great mind a writer,
An author like Rowling or Tolkein,
A playwright like Shakespeare, or
A poet like Blake?

Is a great mind an artist,
A painter like van Gogh or Monet,
A composer like Mozart, or
A famous pop musician?

Animals have great minds,
They have learned to evolve and endure,
Some have taught themselves to migrate,
And, once they have found something works, they stick to it.

If humans were forced to live like animals,
We would fall apart,
We have forgotten our distant past,
We have forgotten nature.

We have forgotten we were once one of *them,*
We have forgotten we are equal,
Evolution gave us an advantage,
Yet some people use this for prejudice and evil.

Our world thrives on boundaries and knowledge,
Not on physical fitness,
Our race is getting weaker,
Our emotions mean that the weak survive with the strong.

Animals have emotions too,
They feel it when they are caged, tortured and killed.

Harriet Mchale-Owen (12)
Rugby High School, Rugby

School Sounds!

Boys shout,
Girls giggle,
Pencils go squiggle, squiggle.

Bell goes,
All out,
The teacher is Mr Sprout.

Chatter, laughter,
Hands clap,
Skipping rope goes slap, slap.

Football thuds,
Conkers bash,
Hear the chemistry window smash!

Apples are crunched,
Sweets are eaten.
Hear the bell rung by Mr Beaton.

Back in the classroom,
Stuffy and hot,
Listen for today's lunch bubbling in the pot.

Lunch eventually arrives,
Hear the shouts and screams,
Also hear the teacher's dress rip at the seams!

The day has ended,
No children, not even a magpie,
Teachers hold their breath and then they sigh!

Emily Vincent (11)
Rugby High School, Rugby

The Greatest Animal

When people say,
'Who was the greatest mind?'
They automatically think,
A scientist? An artist? The blind?

All people are great
And some take the glory,
But the greatest
Are those beyond the story.

They are the ones, the ones that do not tell,
They don't shout about their inventions,
They cannot speak our language
Or get our attention.

The memory of a goldfish,
Is this really fair?
As sick as a pig,
I thought you said you care!

Dogs are *man's best friend,*
But you still say,
As mad as a dog -
At least once a day.

So why do you take the trouble
To offend the animals
When really they are the greatest minds
Out of all the mammals?

Kayleigh Gray (13)
Rugby High School, Rugby

Who Has The Greatest Mind?

We were told to write a poem,
With the theme of greatest minds,
I thought about it carefully
And here is what I did find.

You could say that Newton,
The physicist, topped them all,
He realised that it was gravity
That made his apple fall.

You could say that Dickens,
The author, was hard to beat,
To write so many novels
Was certainly no mean feat.

You could say that Columbus,
The explorer, had a great mind,
He proved the world was round,
And the New World he did find.

But the more I thought about it,
It all seemed so clear,
Another person with a great mind
Was standing very near.

Think of all the things I know
And all the places I could go,
All the choices I could make
And all the chances I could take,
Although my mind may not be the best,
In its hands my future rests.

Megan Jacob (12)
Rugby High School, Rugby

Great Minds

My dad says that great minds think alike.
Is it true then that when
Albert Einstein used to ride his bike,
He came up with the ideas about the speed of light?
While Edison worked on electricity,
It was in his lab where Einstein thought about relativity.

It was at this time when Marie Curie discovered radiation,
While Wilbur and Orville studied aviation.

Considering Galileo was blind,
He worked with science of every kind.
He studied stars and planets alike,
But wasn't really the mechanical type.

This he left to Leonardo,
Who came up with methods of shifting cargo.
His ideas were way ahead of his time,
The helicopter being the first of the line.

This all shows my dad is wrong,
That great minds don't all think alike
Because if they did, then we'd all be singing the same song!

Lauren Knights (13)
Rugby High School, Rugby

Dressing Up

On Monday I was a princess,
So I had a pink castle and a sparkly crown.
On Tuesday I was a monkey,
So I ate nothing but bananas and hung upside down.

On Wednesday I was a fairy,
So I flapped my wings and flashed my wand.
On Thursday I was a goldfish,
So I went deep-sea diving and explored the pond.

On Friday I was a grown-up,
So I wore shiny high heels and tidied the house.
On Saturday I was a cat,
So I played in the garden and chased a mouse.

On Sunday I was a mermaid,
So I flipped my green tail and brushed my long hair.
Then the time just flew by,
And I don't really care.

Now I live in a flat, with a view of the dump,
My kids are a pain and my boyfriend's a lump.
I don't like my job and I'm out of ideas,
My great mind's killed dead and I'm bored to tears.

Lindsey Frodsham (13)
Rugby High School, Rugby

Great Minds

William Shakespeare
Wrote poems and plays
In the time of the Tudors,
Won Elizabeth's praise.

Peter Tchaikovsky,
Russian composer,
Wrote the 'Nutcracker Suite',
Played over and over.

Elizabeth Tudor,
Magnificent queen
Not ruled by men,
She was painted serene.

Charles Darwin
Thought of how we began,
And how we evolved
From monkey to man.

A musician, a monarch,
A writer of plays,
A thinker; their wisdom
Passed on for an age.

Ella Horne (13)
Rugby High School, Rugby

Simple People But Great Minds

Not only scientists and writers
Have great minds stored in their heads
We only think of famous minds
But what about simple people instead?

Teachers, doctors and firefighters
All have large brains too,
They use them till they expand and almost explode
To help people like me and you.

Why do simple people get overlooked
When they help us so much through life?
Just think about what they must go through,
People causing trouble and strife.

Firefighters save our lives,
Doctors make us better,
Teachers teach us everything
Right down to the last letter.

So if they do such good things,
Why aren't their talents shown?
Why don't we give something back for once
And make simple but great minded people well-known.

Hannah Gamble (13)
Rugby High School, Rugby

Mind Of A Monkey

My mind is the greatest of all,
But such a shame nobody else knows.
Those insolent humans that go past my cage every day,
Don't even realise that I can understand everything they say.
Who are they playing at when they pull faces at me?
Some brainless person said I'm not very good looking.
Is that why?
Have they ever looked in the mirror?
No wonder nobody wants to look at them.

My mind is the greatest of all,
It's just that I'm confined to a cage and they're not.
The reason for it is that I keep my fur but they shave it off.
My IQ must be higher than that of the person they call Einstein.
I have beauty and brains,
But still, why does no one realise that I have the greatest mind of all?

Ushna Qureshi (13)
Rugby High School, Rugby

Tribute!

It's not the same without him!
I saw him,
I fell in love with him,
And I lost him!

He was mine,
I thought he'd never leave me,
I was wrong!

I hugged him,
I cried into his fur,
And I watched him go!

It broke my heart,
Part of me was missing,
But he will always be in my mind!
It's not the same without him!

Emma Chamberlain (12)
Rugby High School, Rugby

The Way It Is

It seemed like a good idea then
The sun shone down on me that day
The day I first met you
I looked your way, you smiled at me,
And that was how it began.
Smiling, laughing, talking, sharing,
Slowly building a friendship
That I hoped might become something more.

But I saw you with her tonight
In this cold, unfamiliar place
And my dreams of us crumbled
At the same moment as my heart.
Whoever would have thought
My good idea would end this way
With you happily in love with her
And I still standing all alone?

Sarah Garland (11)
Rugby High School, Rugby

Victims With Great Minds

In the corner they sit
With their heads in their hands
Trying to think
And start a new plan
To get away from the end of the day
Where there's pain and sorrow, come what may
But still they stay strong and do not give in.

So in the corner they sit
Getting on with the class
Talking to friends in the middle of maths
But they know there is something they must do
So they go to the head's office and tell them who
Caused pain and suffering, they did not give in.

Amy Mellor (13)
Rugby High School, Rugby

Great Minds

No one has ever seen a mind,
We just assume it's there.
Never a moment without it shall pass,
An infinite fountain of thoughts.

A mind is a very special gift,
It opens many doors.
The passageways of knowledge and hope,
To discover the splendours of life.

Scientific minds, artistic minds,
Music and medicine too.
Diversity, the spice of life
That moulds and shapes our world.

Dreams, secrets and fears,
All locked up in your head.
Our minds hold the key to answers,
We just have to unlock the door.

Laura Mahon (13)
Rugby High School, Rugby

Broken Dreams

B oulevard of broken dreams,
R eality is far away,
O nly broken dreams can enter
K eep them safe from nightmares, pray,
E ver roaming to and fro,
N ever leave, they have to stay.

D reams are special, personal,
R emember, they're yours to keep,
E nsure that you are kind to them,
A nd they will help you sleep.
M any dreams are broken though
S o they go to the boulevard to weep.

Becci Postins (12)
Rugby High School, Rugby

Great Minds

The dying, the poor,
The people fighting in the war,
The shooting, the guns,
The people see, they scream and run.
The bomb and the dynamite,
At least they didn't see the sight.
The bodies, the blood,
Dead children lying in the mud,
The murder and the genocide,
Hitler and his suicide,
The racism and prejudice,
It's all something we want to miss.
And all of this came from the brain,
The suffering, the waves of pain,
From the working of a great mind,
But the things it does to humankind . . .

Sophie Meakin (13)
Rugby High School, Rugby

Creation

Different seasons,
What are the reasons?
Cold air flushes,
Sensational hot rushes,
From falling snow on the ground
To autumn trees' rustling sound.

Our beautiful world so warm and neat,
Even when there's tumbling sleet.
From animals so cuddly and cute
To pretty melodies from a flute.
Thank you God for all you made
From bunches of grapes to lemonade!

Rhiannon Walls (12)
Rugby High School, Rugby

Dreams

Mind's core
       Where secrets
  Dwell
     Never
To be
   Unlocked.

Magically surreal
         And
More precious
        Than
All the
   Treasures in

The whole world.

The stark truths
        Of our souls
Revealed
    Peering into the
Deepest
    Darkest
Crevices of
      Our hearts
We are
   Laid bare

The ambitions
      That shape
Our existence
     Are . . .

  . . . Dreams.

Rajkiran Barhey (12)
Rugby High School, Rugby

Great Minds

As vibrant as a shadow in the mist,
As significant as a dewdrop in the storm,
Faded apparently perfectly into the scenery,
Hidden behind the camouflage of my skin,
These friends' voices crack the hollows of my tones,
With flamboyant animated tales,
Great tales from great minds.

And still I try to continue with a lively anecdote,
But laughter overrides my melancholic mood,
And my salty springs silently slip into the joyous uproar too,
Each one unique, as they drip to the floor,
Lowly tears from a lowly mind.

I edge from the crowd unnoticed; isolated from popularity,
Isolated for longing to be part,
A nobody thrown accidentally into a world of somebodies,
A lowly thought drowning in a sea of great minds.

Emma-Louise Page (15)
Rugby High School, Rugby

The Protector

You fly so swiftly beside me,
You glide so high in the air,
I am bewildered when I see you,
But hardly notice you are there.

You are like my companion,
Gliding through the night,
You protect me when I'm sleeping,
By day, you stick by me with might.

Sometimes I can't see you,
But I always believe you are there,
Flying so swiftly beside me,
Gliding so high in the air.

Catherine Alsworth (11)
Rugby High School, Rugby

A New School

I'm getting ready - so excited
I'm leaving home - really nervous
I'm meeting my friends - very pleased
I'm walking towards school - enthusiastic
I'm entering the gates - *petrified!*

I'm in . . .

I'm passing the older students - feeling so small
I'm looking at the teachers - so important
I'm walking down the corridor - am I lost?
I'm arriving at my form room - very nice.

I'm in . . .

I'm talking to my classmates - so lucky
I'm making new friends - very glad
I'm thinking about home - unhappy
I'm waiting for the teacher - hope she's nice.

She's in . . .

I'm going to my lesson - slightly shy
I'm reading a book - very good
I'm doing my work - quite hard
I'm finishing it off - thankful
I'm leaving the school - grateful

I'm out . . .

I'm walking home - very relieved
I'm entering the garden - very happy
I'm unlocking the door - thrilled

I'm in . . .

Fiona Briggs (12)
Rugby High School, Rugby

Emotions

Joyful emotions
Overwhelm me
Lifting
Off the ground
Hear
My heart bursting
With happiness
Flying
Like the stars
On a silver night
Glittering
In the moonlight
Entrancing up . . . up . . . up

Suddenly stopped
Kicked
Murdered
Light in my heart
Dims slowly
Regains itself gently
Comes for revenge
Loathing it with hatred
Trying not to retort
Two evil eyes
Awaiting a challenge
Cannot keep this abuse
Save me . . .
Please!

Janeeth Devgun (12)
Rugby High School, Rugby

Bastogne

The snow crunched under our feet as we entered the forest.
Our mission was simple: stop the Nazis from taking Bastogne.
As I looked over enemy lines, I felt all alone.
So many of them, so few of us - the word impossible echoed
in my mind.
I thought, almost knew that I was going to die in this fight.
It was not so much the task of digging that wore us all out -
It was the slow realisation that we might not see home again.
I had been digging for what felt like a week, in snow, fog and ice.
My foxhole had logs for a roof - probably not enough to save me.

The shelling that I had feared started at first light on Boxing Day.
All around me were screams of panic, fear and slow but definite death.
I watched from my foxhole as two men from my company were hit.
I ducked down into the small space, fearing for my life.
Captain Tompkins, an officer, called to me
He told me that we were moving to Bastogne to fight for the town.
I jumped out of my hiding place and followed the captain to the others.
My company, Easy Company, moved into the town first.
It was always the case: first into battle, last ones out.
We ran to the closest house and hid behind it.
I signalled to the rest of the battalion to join us.
We moved in on the enemy, coming from behind, firing as we went.
They turned and in their thousands returned fire.
We battled on for hours, firing shells, bullets and whatever else
we could.
Eventually after days of heavy fighting, the Germans surrendered.
We returned to the rear, a place to rest, eat and have a hot shower.

Before the battle, I thought I was going to die, so much I almost
knew it.
I hadn't died; in fact I hadn't even come close to death.
I learnt more in that battle than I learnt in the whole war:
Trust in your company, trust in your friends, trust in your officer,
But most of all, trust in yourself.

Elizabeth Barnes (12)
Rugby High School, Rugby

Chicken

I see the birds,
Flapping, flying, free,
How I long to be free,
All I do all day is work,
Laying, pecking, wishing.
There must be something beyond these walls.
I'm trapped,
I can't flap or fly, I'm not free.
How much I wish I could spread my wings and escape,
Maybe when we were created, they missed off a part,
The part that makes it possible to fly.
Well, you can't have everything.
People don't do much thinkin'
For a fed up chicken.

Which came first,
The chicken
Or the egg?
For all I know, the eggs never hatch,
He takes them away
Into the deep, dark blackness.
I wonder where I came from,
I'll probably never know.
Live, eat, die,
All in this place,
It is not life,
It is slavery,
People don't do much thinkin'
For a fed up chicken.

Helen Butler (12)
Rugby High School, Rugby

The Day My Goldfish
Took Over The Universe . . .

The day my goldfish took over the universe
Is a day I will never forget,
He crashed through the house and stole my purse,
And buying him I regret.

I was cleaning him out when his ordeal began,
He swelled to the size of a hot air balloon,
He spoke in gobbledegook like no man
And floated up to the moon.

He came back down with a terrible crash,
And broke my roof in two,
When he came up, he had grown a moustache,
It was so absurd; I couldn't believe it was true.

Muttering all the way, upstairs he went,
And into my bathroom,
On his back he carried a tent
And, in his fin, he held a broom.

At the same time my mum came through the door,
A pin in her outstretched arm,
She shrieked at the awful sight she saw,
That she nearly set off the alarm.

She went upstairs in an awful flap,
Following my fish fin,
And there she found him, standing by a tap,
So she pricked him with a pin.

Immediately he deflated into any old pet,
And that was the end of that,
But did I tell you that I once met
A horse dancing on a hat?

Lucy Elliott (12)
Rugby High School, Rugby

Down A Country Lane

Down a country lane,
Where no cars pass me by,
I hear the sounds of nature,
Birds' sweet songs,
Bumbling, buzzing bees,
Cows mooing, I smell their presence too,
The beautiful little lambs springing about, bleating for their mothers.
My eyes are drawn by the sweet-smelling primroses growing
in the hedgerow,
Where little robin redbreast is building her nest.
The clouds float by,
Briefly covering the sun,
But soon the glistening gold sunrays are beaming brightly down again,
Warming my whole body.
A horse and rider comes trotting by,
Hooves clipping on the lane.
My senses feel refreshed,
By this weekend escape from the hubbub noise of town.

Catherine Cemery (12)
Rugby High School, Rugby

Love

A trip from reality,
The ride of a lifetime,
A rose-tinted vision of life.

Swept away in a whirlwind,
Your heart's all a-flutter,
You want it to last forever.

It consumes you,
Caresses you,
Nothing can stop this
For it is love.

Louise Fleming (11)
Rugby High School, Rugby

Great Minds

Inside our head we each have a brain,
Generating thoughts without restraint,
Every minute of every day,
100 billion neurones are ticking away.

There are those whose minds are methodical and slow,
Their ideas are fertile and continue to grow.
Others think in bursts - like frisky grasshoppers.
Their ideas explode suddenly - like party poppers!

But what is it that makes a mind great?
What are the features of that Einstein trait?
Is it the ability to remember this and that
Or to have original thoughts at the drop of a hat?

Works of art or scientific inventions
All require minds of enormous dimensions.

However, in the midst of all this confusion,
This poem has finally reached its conclusion:
The factors that contribute to a great mind
Cannot always be clearly defined!

Claudia Clarke (13)
Rugby High School, Rugby

Books (Haiku)

A book is a train,
Your thoughts make you your ticket,
Your mind is the track.

Harriet Dainty (11)
Rugby High School, Rugby

A Storm In A Maths Lesson

There's a storm in the maths lesson brewing
Today, that's what we've all learnt
The lightning has ruined the textbooks
And the pie charts are looking rather burnt.

Mr Walker can't speak for the thunder
The clouds make the fittings quite damp
The clock has stopped working; *kaput!*
We're all looking like homeless tramps.

Long division is reduced to smudges
The rain's coming down in sheets
The classroom's ablaze with blue light
We're sheltering under our seats.

The compasses are getting rusty
The electric whiteboard's giving off sparks
The units of measurement gone to slush
You can't tell the squares from the arcs.

The storm is subsiding although it still rains
When the bell goes we run, flee
By the time we reach humanities
There's a rainbow in history.

Daisy Woolham (12)
Rugby High School, Rugby

Another School Day

School gates open,
children run in
as a new school day
starts again.

Boys talk,
girls chat,
nitter-natter, yak, yak, yak!
Pencils write,
squiggle, squiggle.
Get it wrong,
rub it out,
break bell's gone,
everyone get out!

Footballs bounce,
hands clap,
skipping ropes
hit the floor and slap.
Boys play tig,
girls do handstands,
a ball gets thrown and lands on Mrs Figg.
Teacher gets cross,
as she rings the bell.
Ring, ring!
Sad faces plod in.

All quiet,
not a sound.
You can hear a
pin drop on the ground.
As the teacher's lesson comes to an end,
the bell rings for home time,
glory be!
Mum has saved me from another school day!

Rosie Anderson (11)
Rugby High School, Rugby

People These Days

'People these days,' he said with a giggle,
'Always the youngsters who wiggle and wriggle!'
'I don't know,' came her reply,
'It's always the elders who give up a sigh!'
'Agreed, I know,' the old lady said,
'Though, 'tis the politicians whose speeches we dread!'
'All thoughts considered,' her husband agreed,
'But doctors and nurses cause us to bleed.'
'Ah ha, I see,' a passer-by called,
'But men are known to always be bald.'
'Right, that's true,' a male friend smiled,
'But women are only for watching their child.'
'That is correct,' a teacher threw back,
'But it always seems that bosses must sack.'
'Sure, I can see,' a divorcee added,
'But lovers have their partners abraded . . .'
'That's obvious,' a baby babbled,
'And parents don't care when you're all dabbled.'
'I suppose that's right,' a parent admitted,
'But babies are never, ever permitted!'
'Yup,' the skater spluttered his words,
'But the picked on people are always the nerds!'
The nerd piped in, 'I agree, good chum,
But better be picked on than to be dumb!'
They bickered and bickered for yonders it seemed,
Until finally I decided and I went and I screamed!
Eventually I could say, 'Yes, I see,
If I can't be these things, what can I be?'
'Yeah, people these days,' they said as a game,
'We suppose they are all the same!'

Samantha Driscoll (12)
Rugby High School, Rugby

The Vacuum Cleaner's Revenge

I woke up to a normal day;
I went down to start my chores.
I unearthed Snozzle the vacuum cleaner,
Out from Dad's old stores.

I pressed the switch to make him go,
He started with a roar;
Then, before I could stop him,
He was out the kitchen door!

I heard a high-pitched woman's scream
Coming from over the wall,
I climbed up on the barbecue
And was transfixed at what I saw:

By her own back door
Mrs Hettage was cowering
Whilst Snozzle advanced upon her,
His nozzle violently spinning.

He reared back on his castors,
The cable nearly hit me;
The garden looked like a bomb site -
It looked like World War III.

I groaned and jumped over,
Grabbed him by the tail;
Dragged him into our garden
And tied him to the clothes rail.

Inside I slumped on the sofa;
Trying to calm my brain:
I jumped up to the ghastly shout -
'The vacuum's loose again!'

Amy Down (11)
Rugby High School, Rugby

The Monday Morning Curse

Could there be anything worse
Than the Monday morning curse?
It starts a very dull day for me,
I have to get up awfully early.
I eat my breakfast and wash my face,
I clean my teeth and to my disgrace,
I have to get ready for school!

School isn't my favourite place,
And I'd rather get ready at a snail's pace.
But no, I have to get dressed,
And pack my bag! Oh what a pest!
And then sadly I get on my shoes and coat,
'I don't have to go yet,' my sister gloats.
Then I have to get on the bus.

The bus always smells on a Monday,
Of disinfectants they put on it on Sunday.
It goes through the town to other places,
Past working people with big briefcases.
And then it stops,
I get off the bus then I sigh,
Oh dear, Friday afternoon is not very close by!

So could there be anything worse
Than the Monday morning curse?

Sarah Elizabeth Farthing (11)
Rugby High School, Rugby

The Beach In Grand Cayman

As I step out of the car, collecting my things, ready for the beach;
My toes are tickled by soft white sand that stretches out for miles;
The sun is beating down on me, although I am protected by suncream
And the sea is in front of me, the gentle waves rolling in and out,
                       an inviting clear-blue cooling sensation.
People are dotted here and there, on the sand or in the sea;
A soft breeze makes my hair dance around my head as I watch and
                       take in the beach in Grand Cayman.

As I walk across the sand, I place my umbrella for some shade
                       against the sun,
And I jump into the sea and instantly cool down.
I look around underwater and I see thousands of shells lying on
                       the seabed.
I swim a little further out, where there is a reef.
Schools of tropical fish in all colours and sizes swim and then
                 they change direction when I stretch out my arm.
Dozens of sea plants come into my view, and I realise how pretty
                       the beach in Grand Cayman really is.

Time to go home now and what a shame it is to leave the beautiful
Caribbean beach that I have spent the day in, enjoying myself.

Christina Constantinides (12)
Rugby High School, Rugby

Divorce

Parents shouting, stamping their feet on the floor
While their child listens outside the door
The noise echoes in her head for evermore
Divorce

Upstairs in her room the child cries
She's sick of all her parents' lies
Her face is hot and tears blind her eyes
Divorce

She goes to school the very next day
She is still upset but she will not say
She doesn't think they'd care anyway
Divorce

A month later the dad has moved out
There is no more screaming, not even a shout
The child wanders aimlessly about
Divorce

Her eyes have big purple bags and her face is white
Years later she remembers her parents' spite
She has not yet recovered from the fight
The consequences of divorce.

Natasha Wilson (12)
Rugby High School, Rugby

Istanbul City Of Dreams

City of azure waters and stalagmite minarets,
Priceless Byzantine treasures and crusader threats.
Chanting muezzins call the faithful to prayer,
Sightseers: shuffling snakes with somnambulating stare.
Every invader, emperor and vizier,
Attempted to recreate Heaven here
By intrigue, statecraft, inheritance or fear,
Forever remoulded and reborn for a grand desire
Accompanied by fluorescent sunsets of Technicolor fire.

Scenes of battles, bloodshed and lust
A chameleon of cultures, perfidy and mistrust.
First Constantinople, then Byzantium, now Istanbul
A whirling dervish in time's whirlpool.
The timeless enchantment of the Grand Bazaar:
A barrage of sights, smells, sounds, spices from afar.
Glittering fabrics for the harem walls and palaces,
Fluttering butterflies on flower-filled terraces
The magic mystery of the veiled women hidden behind the walls;
Snatches of mournful songs, cascades of rippling laughter.

Nut-brown urchins in jostling, swift feral packs
Hunt down coins between moving feet, oblivious to kicks and smacks
Shouted insults ricochet over the heaving human crater
Silence like the cool, glittering, domed cavern of Hagia Sophia.
Take away cars, buses, the droning incessant radio beat,
Return petal-strewn gardens, carved jewelled mosques
Blinding white-finger minarets
Pointing skyward in the still, dry heat.
The hum of the Bazaar and the chant of the prayer caller
A shimmering swish of black veil
Disappearing around a corner
Sights and sounds that echo through eternity
Only thinly papered by modernity.

Venetia Congdon (13)
The Cheltenham Ladies' College, Cheltenham

Egyptian Marketplace

I could see the ancient pyramids looming in the distance
Whilst I was at the bazaar.
As I walked through the bustling crowds,
I breathed heavily in the dry heat.

It was easy to imagine the country in its former glory.
It was easy to picture the pharaohs worshipping at the temples.
I could shut my eyes and be taken back
To a time when everything was different.

The marketplace is in its own separate world,
As soon as I entered I was overwhelmed by the sights and smells.
The donkeys, hagglers and dusty earth
Made me think I was being submerged in the past.

The stalls were laden with all sorts of things
From intricate handmade carpets, to chunky gold bracelets:
The aisles were crammed with exquisite little finds
The treasures that I will never forget.

But, even if I stole a quick glance at a stall
The stallholder would come rushing over to me.
Knowing I was a foreigner, he would babble in English
About something beautiful I should buy from him.

The marketplace became daunting;
The hagglers persistent and ferocious.
I was so lucky to be there but
I was intimidated.

Katarina Kennedy (14)
The Cheltenham Ladies' College, Cheltenham

Ode To Paris

Paris
You are my dream city
Every lover's domain
A haven of culture

Your name inspires images of
The Seine carving its meandering path
Young lovers strolling hand in hand
Cafés spilling onto your streets

An underlying sense of restlessness exists
Bustling with life that's hard to suppress
A feeling of purpose and yet of indolence
You exude a general 'joie de vivre'

The great architects of your past have left their mark
Gustav Eiffel one
Although long gone, his tower remains
Standing proud, surveying its realm

Your grand, tree-lined boulevards
Disguise a consumer's paradise
Exquisite jewellery, delicate fragrances
Fashions of the catwalk

Paris
Your charms are indisputable
Your zest for life unquestionable
My heart will be yours forever.

Nicola Jee (15)
The Cheltenham Ladies' College, Cheltenham

Ode To Hong Kong

City of glowing lights,
a small pinpoint on a vast globe,
within the clutches of proud mountains
which stand tall on their territory,
absorbing the excited hubbub below.

In a world of your own
you reflect the hot rays with which the sun torments you,
trapping me in a golden haze
that I cannot escape.

Your purity envelopes me,
though not so pure,
a mist hangs over us,
an ever nearing cloud of the undiscovered
that stretches over,
holding the emerald sea hostage.

I admire your everlasting power
that grips at those who indulge in your empire,
outlining us from childhood to your dutiful height,
we enter the unknown.

A sparkling jewel,
pulsating forever inside me.
I will not forget,
my gratitude is eternally yours.

Francesca Waldron (15)
The Cheltenham Ladies' College, Cheltenham

The Moors

The train is rumbling slowly, unhurriedly,
through the Devon countryside.
There isn't much to see outside.
It's mainly just fields of brown and grey and green.
There isn't much to be seen.

Until eventually,
the train begins to slow down and suddenly,
we are leaning upwards.
People hold onto their seats as the train accelerates.
I wonder where we are going.

Peering out of my grimy train window,
I see the boring fields left behind.
Then like Earth being chipped away
like a carpenter and a block of wood
there they are - the moors of Devon.

They are spread below us like a quilt,
sheltered by a rocky border.
There is nothing to stop the train falling,
just some scrubby grass and a few loose stones.
I imagine that I am falling through the air,
but the quilt below engulfs me and stops my fall.

Wild ponies run past the train, they look
angry to see such a metal monstrosity
running through their homes.
Their hooves fly up high in the air,
as if they are going to jump onto the train.
But the train gives a surge of energy and the horse is lost.

All too soon we are back at the station.
The trip is over, but I will remember
the places I have been and the things I have seen.

Lily Shepherd (12)
The Cheltenham Ladies' College, Cheltenham

If I Were . . .

If I were princess of Poelisie,
Fine gowns and jewels I'd wear
And every prince would fall for me,
With my crown upon my golden hair.

If I were princess of Tellereau,
I think I'd have a horse
And together we'd win every jumping show
And I'd have lots of medals, of course.

If I were princess of Miramar,
Gold bangles I would keep,
My future would shine like a glowing star,
As I dreamt of it in my sleep.

If I were princess of Angelahark,
Every week I'd give a music show,
I'd sing as beautifully as a lark,
And I'd play the violin and the piano.

If I were princess of Posalind,
I'd be slim and pretty too,
I'd be a gymnast and rather loose-limbed
And be busy with lots to do.

If I were princess of anywhere,
I would be all of these things,
But as I'm not a princess of here or there
I'll forget about my dreams.

Olivia Brown (11)
The Cheltenham Ladies' College, Cheltenham

Laughter

When the awful thing starts,
It's just one person, trying to hide it.
The teacher sucks in her breath
And hopes that nobody else has noticed.

But to her utter dismay,
The ghastly child decides that she'll laugh again.
Although this time it's a little louder,
But still, nobody seems to have caught the disease yet.

The teacher's sharp little eyes begin to scan the room.
At the back of the class the affected child
Is trying to cover up her laughs.
Now other children are looking up and smiling
The teacher starts to talk double fast to distract them.

It seems to work at first
But then the teacher slips and says something rude.
That means trouble!
The whole class is looking shocked, but they're not laughing yet!

But then that dratted girl starts to laugh again.
Now she's really in trouble
One by one the disease spreads to every girl in the room
All the girls are laughing and some are even falling off their chairs.

The teacher screams and pulls her hair,
'I should have got rid of that stupid girl at the start, it's not fair!'
Suddenly the disease is cured.
Silence, at last!

Sophie Gearing (12)
The Cheltenham Ladies' College, Cheltenham

Happiness Is Everywhere

Laughter is a memory,
Of happy days you've had.
And if there was no laughter,
Then your life's memory will be bad.

At school we laugh like mad
At friends who slip and fall
And even though it might have hurt them,
None of us care at all.

If a friend does something funny
And you react by laughing loud
It shows that you're enjoying yourself
And should do your fun heart proud.

If you watch a funny film,
For example Will and Grace,
Do you laugh at what they did
Or because they pulled a face?

Can you remember the last time you laughed
And what it was all about?
Do you laugh now as much as you did
Or do you not laugh and just have a pout?

When you see something hilarious
And you don't want to show it's funny
Do you sort of smile and grin
Until it pops inside your tummy?

Personally, I think laughing and smiling
Is a good way to enjoy yourself
So every so often laugh and smile
Because by now you should know it's *ace!*

Emily Sumaria (12)
The Cheltenham Ladies' College, Cheltenham

In The Jungle

Rumbling through the forest along a bumpy road
The smell of fresh rain sitting on the leaves
The sound of the Venus flytrap snapping its jaws
The call of the parrot to its love
The reply in a sweet, high song
The scuttling of insects racing to the rocks
The scream and shout of my brothers and sisters
The purr of the Jeep's engine
The smell of fruits dropped by their tree
The feel of the thick, dense air against pale skin
The taste of the natural spices on my tongue
The malodorous smell the dung beetles produce
The squeak of the suspension
The wheels spinning up dust
The rustle of the trees in the slight winds
The careful footsteps of an animal about to pounce
The tinkling of running water
The dusty, humid air filling my lungs
The leaves floating to the ground with the season's change
The breeze brushing past my face
The cracking of sticks as predators walk
The big yellow eyes of a bush baby
The peacefulness of the forest
The crackly noise of the radio
The feel of the chilled cool box below your feet
The sign of which winding path to take next
The sun's rays beating down on the back of necks
The stillness becomes unearthly
The sounds become distant
The tastes become sour
The smells become ghastly
And then a shot . . .

Amy Sumaria (13)
The Cheltenham Ladies' College, Cheltenham

Final Journey

The light glimmering ahead is drawing me on
Through these dark tunnels.
The smell of death is thick
Penetrating my lungs, forcing me to breathe it in.

The cool air stings my nostrils
Catching the breath in my throat
My legs feel like lead and I want to go back
But some unknown force is driving me on.

A wind from nowhere whips at my ragged clothing,
Torn from the journey here.
The walls are slimy, wet and cold,
Is it wet with blood or water?
I do not know.

I don't know where I am going, but I cannot stop.
The light is close now, so close I could reach out
And touch it,
But my hand stays at my side.

I can make out a big wooden door
In the blinding white light.

The door slowly opens
My whole body feels warm now.
Relief seeps through me to my bones
Easing all pain.

With no hesitation
I step inside the door,
Knowing that I am in a place of eternal light and happiness.

My memories of life
Will never haunt me again.

Elizabeth Tetley (13)
The Cheltenham Ladies' College, Cheltenham

Ski

The views of towering mountains,
The crackle of the deep new snow,
The warmth of the scarf around me
As the cold breeze started to blow.

I start slowly down the monstrous mountain,
Curving slightly from left to right,
Watching experts whizzing down beside me,
Spraying soft, cool snow in my blurred sight.

Those clumsy snowboarders
Thundering past
Laughing and shrieking
And howling a blast.

I speed down the slopes
I leap over a jump
I find myself tumbling
And landing with a bump.

My warm gloves,
Suddenly filled with snow
And I realise I am covered
In smooth slush from head to toe.

In need of a rest, I board a chairlift
Stretching my legs as I lift my head high.
The smell of pine trees tickles my senses
As I gaze ahead at the peaks of meringue
Touching the sky.

The aroma of steaming hot chocolate
Drifts towards me
As I long for the smooth soft drink
Creamy and frothy.

I love the swoosh and swish of skiing,
As I zigzag through the snow,
I feel the icy swirling flakes
That keep my cheeks aglow.

Gigi Fateh-Iravani (14)
The Cheltenham Ladies' College, Cheltenham

Laughter

Here we are sitting down,
drinking a cup of tea,
and all of a sudden, up it comes,
a spurt of laughter from me.

Creeping up from the tip of my toes,
all the way up to my mouth,
a big spurt of laughter
at a *very* serious time.

You get no warning,
and only the result,
and oh, how good it feels,
to let it all out.

A big, dramatic explosion
coming deep down from me,
a very embarrassing moment,
all from one little thing,
    Laughter!

Zeinab Weyers (12)
The Cheltenham Ladies' College, Cheltenham

Tropical Breath, A Childhood Memory

The ochre sunlight dissolved on our bodies
Lathering us golden-brown
The luminous skies above exposed
A glowing orb sweating down.

The hungry ocean gulped at the beach
Frothy waves licked thirsty feet
Lapping shore and swigging sand
Swelling and sighing to a whimsical beat.

The sizzling white crush of sugar grit sand
Our infectious laughter when hand in hand
Oceanic eyes mirrored dancing sea
Running the beach, my sister and me.

Hannah Salter (16)
The Cheltenham Ladies' College, Cheltenham

Morning Mayhem

'Why are mornings so unpleasant?'
I ask myself every day.
Why was I dragged from my night-time nest
Where I so peacefully lay?

As I untangle myself from my duvet
I grumpily try to ignore
All the persuasive thoughts in my mind,
Telling me to rest some more.

The toast pops up from the toaster
With an unnecessarily shrill screech.
I knock over a jug full of milk when
Lunging for cereal with clumsy reach.

But no, the cereal box is empty -
My morning revival denied me
Crossly, I pour a glassful of orange juice
As there is no time for tea.

Instantly, I hear an angry wail,
An earful of sharp abuse,
Each member of the family outraged
As I realise I have finished the juice.

Struggling to find matching white socks
My mother fumes fit to ignite
As she angrily re-irons the skirt that I
Forgot to hang up last night.

The mad dash in the car is no better
Traffic lights obey orders from Hell,
Making us stop at each and every set
I dash into school on the bell.

I run to registration, and I am late
My heart stops and I have a small fit -
I realise it is Wednesday, not Thursday
And I've forgotten my games kit.

What would I give to be back in bed
Curled away from all this hassle?
But then I wouldn't get my morning treat
Of a fattening, breaktime croissant.

Rachael Kirby (14)
The Cheltenham Ladies' College, Cheltenham

Into The Mist

Lift, drop, lift, drop
Again and again, the sound
Of feet, marching feet,
All around.
Down the road we sweep
The red of our capes and
The bronze of our armour
Bright and alive next to the
Chilling, mossy hills and
Forests nearby.
Our golden eagle
Leading us on into the mist.
A beacon to us,
A warning to others.
Swift, silent, deadly,
That is what we are.
The Ninth Roman Legion
That day we marched out
And were lost in the mist
And to this day only Britain's ageing hillside
Will know what became of us.

Emma McBurney (15)
The Cheltenham Ladies' College, Cheltenham

Galatea's Revenge

*(Galatea was a beautiful statue of a perfect woman created by sculptor Pygmallan.
In response to his prayers it was brought to life by Aphrodite the goddess of love)*

His fevered fingers caressed my damp waxen skin;
puckered brow he nipped and tucked at my slender frame
as my cold polished orbs failed to darken to his incandescent desires.
My mouth was bone-dry with anger ignited by his searing hands.
I was the apple of his eye
put on a pedestal, but for the drone of

Pygmalion's infatuated sighs; my
hungry patience was sweetly rewarded
by Aphrodite's drunken complacency.
A goblet of Adam's ale quenched my burning rancour.
Indebted to my creator? No, I was dealt a Lot's luck
by Medusa's forked digits and flung to the

snake pit. The Sculptor suffocated me with rapturous embrace and
rippling gifts, but he hadn't the husbandry to cut and suck the venom,
from the core of my heart. A virginal concept, I only deserved a mirror
for a mate. His sordid hands carved hours of passion with easy marks.
Home he swaggered with the smell of red on his breath. Red-handed.
He dyed me. I was putty in his hands.

Drunk with salacity, he stormed from the room.
That's beyond the pale; I fumed to his ebbing retreat.
Hot salty tears clutched the curves of my
cheeks, while a bitter laugh escaped my alabaster lips.
I rushed to the kitchen. A knife hushed my black humour.
I saw the peace. The severed veins. The blood

thirsty on my chin. It was then I had an idea. Set in
stone. Like a snake in the grass I slithered to his workbench.
That counterfeit creator. That snaky maggot. That
was enough. Pygmalion had made a
mar in calling me his own, for Galatea has a heart of stone.

At the threshold, a riot of consonants he raged towards me but
stopped. Petrified. The look in my eyes transfixed him whilst
with the sleight of my hand I stole his breath and cast it out to the
wind frenzied olive. Only now could I look him in the eye;
a knot of shadow triumphant in the witching hour haunted, the bitter -
sweet aftertaste lingering on my sin;

like his perfumed garments still lying in the bedchamber. His satanic silhouette took a coal-black grip on me, smothering all thoughts of sleep. Even the silence gnawed greedily at my pasty features.

A chip off the old block whispered the erect ebony Pygmalion. I replied with a distracted bark of relief. A white lie rid me of his presence; a car boot sale his form. And now

but for the look on his face I would be at rest.

He plagues me all day and night; his ebony hands devouring my milky skin, massaging my sorry sanity. I see the world now purely in black and white. That I should be dead and he fathering new life. But the stark moon reminds me of the billions of stars slowly dying, cosmoses away. Without voice to mark their husband's judicious gaze. Without release.

Olivia Crellin (15)
The Cheltenham Ladies' College, Cheltenham

Sunshine

The rays,
Outstretched fingers,
Reaching out to veiled niches,
Attempts to enliven the gloom,
Solace

Shimmers,
Light on water
Dancing on the surface,
Unpredictable like dear hopes,
Flickering

Shadows
Creep in sight,
Cloaking the orange streaks
And like the distant chimeras,
It fades.

Catherine Cheng (15)
The Cheltenham Ladies' College, Cheltenham

Ariadne, The Wife Of Dionysus

It was late July. I stood there by the kitchen sink
Waiting for the kettle to boil.
Cradling my ring in the sieve of my hands, as it were
a newborn child. Delicate. Fragile.
Too cowardly to place it on the table,
Afraid that I might leave it there.

The kettle's steamy breath clings to my skin,
Its sweaty hands caressing me.
Faded memories glide across glassy eyes.
Glaring at submissive tears gliding into my coffee
Anger trembles through my body,
Burning through my blood. Sweetly intoxicating. Possessing.

Staring at the adulteress who has stolen my marriage.
Smelling her rich, spicy breath.
Allowing her to seep seductively into my mouth.
Pungent kisses drip down my throat.
Filling my stomach with a hazy glow.

Hearing the wind tear through the cherry blossom outside.
Scattering its golden-pink dust on the grassy floor.
The branches creak like rusty machinery,
tricking me into hearing my husband finally come home.

At last I see him stumble through the door,
His once loving smile now deformed with drink.
Cringing as he grabs my waist,
His decrying mouth scratching my cheek.
His once honeyed kisses, now tainted with vodka.

Calmly watching as he staggers to his lover,
Selfish, swollen fingers outstretched.
Drinking in her sweet poison like nectar,
His defiant, defensive eyes laughing
As I trudge up the stairs
And climb into an empty bed.

Waking up to the sounds of a stranger,
Watching his mouth dribble excuses,
Like a man about to die.
Too fast.
Too short.
Too late.

But now I sit and watch him
He's with his love.
You see, we work together now.
That is why I'm watching him lovingly cradle her now
Smiling as her poison leaks into his veins,
Inside, laughing.

Lara Wiggin (15)
The Cheltenham Ladies' College, Cheltenham

Emotion

The flood comes into me, not much at first,
Then it rushes in, a tsunami of feeling.
For a while it rages, destroying
And making me destroy.
Then it slips away, leaving disaster all over
And myself destroyed.

The storm starts off on the horizon,
Then it rolls into me, a rumble of thunder.
It strikes and the trees bearing
The fruits of my heart
Cower and try to escape
From the lightning's cruel blast.

The dark cloak surrounds me.
The thick, coarse material is uncomfortable,
But it seems to keep me warm.
My boots are weighing me down -
I cannot move my feet,
Yet they feel like they are protecting me.

Alice Greaves (13)
The Cheltenham Ladies' College, Cheltenham

I Hate Surprises

I clearly remember the horror I felt when I first saw my new baby sister.

I could taste the strangeness of those four words rolling about
on the tip of my tongue
long before I could even fathom what she would turn out to be like.

I had crossed out six big squares on the kitchen calendar
with an extra large felt tip pen
for the days that Mummy had been in hospital -
and my mind was in total turmoil.
I didn't understand anything. Nobody explained!

Why wasn't Mummy at home?
Was her stomach still swollen?
Why was Daddy acting so . . . weird?

The house was so quiet even with Daddy buzzing around
doing all the jobs that Mummy would usually do;
But without Mummy -
Who was going to drive me to my ballet lessons?
(Daddy didn't know the way).

Then one day, as if to relieve my inner confusion
Daddy gave me a funny sort of grin
and told my elder brother and I that it was
time we visited Mummy and a new little surprise.

In the tiny perspex box (was perspex the same as glass?)
My new sister lay, wrapped securely in layers of soft white material -
which reminded me of candyfloss.

But the face that I recall
Poking through the midst of white fluffiness was a . . .
mottled, unpeeled potato head.
I had to stand on the tips of my toes
against the unfriendly, rubbery, twice-sterilised, black hospital pedestal
Just so that I could see that tiny thing.

And this was supposed to be my new sister?
How disgusting.

I thought that all babies had golden locks
And wings! Wings!
Why didn't my sister have wings?

I hate surprises.

Joyce Ng (16)
The Cheltenham Ladies' College, Cheltenham

Early Morning

Where are my socks? Where are my trousers? Where are my shoes?
Drink tea, tie hair, find lead.
Grab phone, call dog, lock door.
Initial rush is over, calm has seeped over me
And I'm walking slowly into bliss.
Drift through the village,
Lights glowing, radio humming, baby crying,
Cars rev, milk bottles tinkle, door slams.
I turn the lane, a silence descends.
Suddenly birds call from the trees,
Urging the world to rise and embrace the day.
Their urgency invigorates me.
The mist has not risen yet,
Cool dewy droplets condense on my face,
Teasing my hair, reviving my soul.
I am alive, running to the top of the hill,
Legs pumping, heart pounding, dogs chasing.
I am at the top. I glimpse the world on the cusp of
A brand new day.
I turn home.

Georgia Tongue (15)
The Cheltenham Ladies' College, Cheltenham

Psyche (Mrs Cupid)

A punching, pitiless, golden-tipped arrow is fired
into mortals with gripping pain, till
the fiery passion seeps into their very marrow, and
the circlet of love is sealed
with the sparks of a burning kiss.
Thy job is done.

Lifted by the gentle Zephyr,
I come to this cold golden palace,
befriended by nothing but distress and fear.
Thy rights I have been told and could never disclaim,
while Hope beholds me of this promise old,
you made, bathed in sweet ambrosial dew.

Listen, the endless choir is singing
the sacred song of state and splendour.
Trapped by Jealousy, my sisters begone.
Wrapped with thy golden ringlets and crimson cheek,
dost thou think this
an ill-matched partnership of God and mortal?

By Venus' order, with utmost diligence,
I sorted out Ceres' golden grain, and
collected the royal fleece of every flock.
Tricked by Sleep in the precious box of Queen-like beauty,
I cross the border and come to you, by this wild, scorching, loving
pain, spreading in my heart from which Pleasure descends.

The Duties must be done,
as darts must find their targets.
So, soar away, through the skies,
in the chariot of gold and do thy job.
Bring people of Astray the amber vase of sweet waters,
to tend their starved, drying lips.

When finally, the wind whistles again,
announcing the return of thy golden-winged chariot.
Feelings, a gift of Excitement and Emptiness, once again,
aflame in my heart, while I,
with Pleasure toddling on the way,
welcome you back for this stay.

Tammy Tong (16)
The Cheltenham Ladies' College, Cheltenham

Hera

I swear to tell the truth, the whole truth and nothing but the truth.

Our marriage began and ended in shame,
the sadness in his bird-like eyes brought him to my breast,
his passion took me by surprise
it was by brute force he dragged me down the aisle.
The twinkle in his eye mocking me as I promised myself to him.
As we lay in bed that night, not for the first time,
the contours of his torso teased me, rippling with laughter.

It wasn't long before I became used to it,
that unique, yet universal smell of them.
The pungent penetrating scent of betrayal, smoking me out,
providing me with a veil for my widow's face.

He locked me in the house, left me to wallow in my bed,
their aroma swarming around me, suffocating, oppressing me,
pushing me into my world, where it was his face lying next to me,
not the indentation of his head on the pillow.

For ten years my bed bore his body, sighing at the weight of his power.
The facade he pulled over himself was wiped away like a smear
from the windowpane by sleep.
It was I who watched his hair receding like surrendering troops.
His worries etched on his brow, cracks in a glacier cold, fatal, beautiful.

I saw their hands, like water slither down his throat,
drowning his lungs with fluid, rotting his heart to the core.
I watched their fingers, be-gloved, run through his hair,
then tear through his mind.
Their sickly utterings entrance him, then slowly send him mad.

I hated them for making me hate him,
I could see him crumbling under their touch.
I wouldn't give them the satisfaction,
I kept my eyes on them, arranged accidents.
It's amazing how easy a couple of snakes are to get hold of,
how odd that they managed it up the stairs.

Emma Sykes (15)
The Cheltenham Ladies' College, Cheltenham

The Lines Of My Hand

Four fingers, one thumb,
Five knuckles, one palm,
One nail, still chipped
From a previous harm.
The pens have been held,
The marks have been made,
The stories all told,
Now beginning to fade.
Two scars with two stories,
One new and one old,
The curves of my life,
Etched deep in the fold.
I study the signs
Each way down the track.
So mysterious the code
And no way back.

Louise Foulkes (15)
The Cheltenham Ladies' College, Cheltenham

Emotion

If it were a food it would be honey rolling on your tongue,
                                        sweet and sugary.
If it were a flower it would be bluebells, smelling fragrant in the spring.
If it were a colour it would be pale, soft on the eyes and beautiful.
If it were a smell it would be talcum powder, the smell of new life.
If it were a type of weather it would be sunny with a soft breeze,
sending pleasant shivers down your spine.
If it were a type of clothing it would be a silk top, soft and caring
                                        on your skin.
If it were a beauty product it would be hand cream, sensitive on
                                        chapped and dry hands.
If it were an emotion it would be pleasure.

Alice Wilton-Steer (13)
The Cheltenham Ladies' College, Cheltenham

When The Garden Fled

One morning the garden fled -
The flower buds fell off their stems
And the paint curled from the fence.
The creatures all wept,
The birds stopped singing,
The dog swallowed his bark
And the butterflies plucked the wings
From their backs.

When the garden fled,
It left behind the swing set,
The tricycle and the slide.
The seasons got stuck together,
Winter, summer, autumn and spring.
The house cried
Into the pond,
But the fish suffocated from the salty tears.

On the day that the garden fled,
The villagers gathered at the cemetery to bury it.
The mailbox spat out the post,
While the oak trees shrivelled,
The colour dripped off the pansies
And a hush spread over the village,
Never to be disturbed
Again.

Claudia Buck (13)
The Cheltenham Ladies' College, Cheltenham

If I Were A Mermaid . . .

If I were a mermaid
I'd glide through the sea
I'd watch the people staring at the quay
I'd lie on the sunny rocks
And watch the ships in the docks.

If I were a mermaid
I'd have glistening rainbow scales
I'd swim with gigantic whales
I'd explore the open blue
I'd always have something to do.

If I were a mermaid
I'd be the queen of the sea beneath
I'd wear a dazzling pink coral wreath
And shells in my fair hair
I'd travel the ocean with not a care.

Rosamund Gadsden (12)
The Cheltenham Ladies' College, Cheltenham

Long Night

Inside my wooden box
I place
a cloak of fire
its dancing flames
to shield me from the darkness,
a tree of hope
forever growing,
a ring of prayer
to bind me to my faith,
a book
the key
to other lighter worlds
and a handful of my native soil . . .

For night will take its time.

Carys Lawrie (13)
The Cheltenham Ladies' College, Cheltenham

Reflections

It sits, silent and empty
Hung on the wall
A frame of a painting with no subject
Waiting, waiting for the echoing footsteps to approach.
A group of giggling schoolgirls skip past it
Each, as they pass, look at it vainly
Adjusting the one strand of hair that is out of place.
Soon comes a young long-haired man,
Dragging his feet along the tiles
It looks back at him, reflecting his empty eyes
As he wonders how long he can spend in the warm room.
It doesn't see the lady in her wheelchair,
Too low to reach the bottom of the frame,
Whilst she sees reflected the white light illuminating the tiled walls.
It is just a bare piece of glass
That has no mind of its own,
Only reflecting its views of the world.

Honoria Simpson (13)
The Cheltenham Ladies' College, Cheltenham

The Table

The surface of polished mahogany is burning
I can see myself in its sheen,
Like a ghost.

A hundred years of history, hidden in its grain
Memories of things long past are deep within.

Now, it is a table in a dining room,
Adorned by roses.
But once it stood tall and proud,
Whispering in the wind.

Eleanor Parsons (13)
The Cheltenham Ladies' College, Cheltenham

Good Morning

Good morning,
Good morning to the busy cook in her kitchen,
Good morning to Mrs Kalie's housekeeper,
To your pots and plants, buds and bushes.
Good morning to the black gentleman in his tree,
To his morning chorus.
Good morning to the mother and her children,
Good morning to your busy pampering and playing.
Good morning to the newspaper man,
To your musty smell and your barking voice,
To your customers, clasping coffee and checking their wrists.
Good morning,
Good morning school children,
To your larking and laughing and black-buckled shoes.
Good morning to the tramp at the corner,
Good morning to the stiff businesswoman,
Good morning to the workers driving their diggers through the earth.
Good morning,
Good morning to the morning.
To the sun and the clouds.
Good morning.

Sophie Pélissie (13)
The Cheltenham Ladies' College, Cheltenham

John Virtue's London

A vast sweep of sprawling rubbish
Compacted and churned out into identical rows of houses.
The factories send plumes of poison, spuming clouds
That settle over children's playgrounds.
Scattered orange peel breaks the line of the pavement at my feet
I trudge alone through the city that bore me, called me its own,
Stamped its name in my memories and future.
I am one among the millions of my brothers and sisters
That are the life blood of the city,
Crowding the arterial streets and alleys of London.
Uniformly it spreads to the broken horizon,
The sky pierced through with towers,
Blunted by blocks of flats.
Seen from above, there is no patchwork
Sewn by the seasons: only concrete, lovingly blasted.
The brick walls of museums and galleries
Are decorated on the outside only by a vagrant artist,
Splashes of colour all but swallowed up by the encroaching grey,
Like the people.

Isabel Seligman (15)
The Cheltenham Ladies' College, Cheltenham

For Night Intends To Stay With Us A Long Time

Be the first in your street to rise
and throw together pots and pans
in a celebration of sound.
Walk into a café. Any café.
Buy a coffee and a slice of cake.
Sit. Breathe in its steamy incense
and feel the condensation clinging to your face.
Buy a newspaper, buy two, buy three
and read. Read with a smile and an eager eye,
for your ability to do so.
Walk through choking fumes
and the molesting shouts of the traffic
to catch a bus.
Go somewhere. See what you've read,
see what you haven't.
Live it.
Do something different, queer, outrageous,
and do it because you can, not because you want to.
They are then ours forever.
For night intends to stay with us a long time.

Sarah Mold (14)
The Cheltenham Ladies' College, Cheltenham

Good Morning

Good morning!
The first word on the matron's lips.
Good morning! As sunlight shines in and doors slam shut.
Good morning, fellow dorm-mates, eyes weary from little sleep.
Good morning to food on plates, barely noticed in its abundance.
Good morning birds who stole my sleep with their twittering.
Good morning friendly smiles and
Good morning less friendly stares and whispers.
Good morning to you, angry teacher
I'm sorry I'm late, I have an excuse.
Good morning, undeserved detention that I have no time to spare for.
Good morning to my parents -
Good morning!
I wish I could tell them good morning, but I have no time to spare
So good morning lonely phone, unused
And good morning old friends lost.
Through lack of contact . . .
Good morning to you,
Good morning to you,
Good morning to you too!

Greta Healy (14)
The Cheltenham Ladies' College, Cheltenham

American Ground

From a long, tiring flight to an American airport
The cool air-conditioned lounge seemed only a thought
With its air of fatigue and its gentle soothing quietness
This space, so empty, such peaceful silence.

A little drinks machine buzzed quietly in the corner
The space was so welcoming, I wanted to stay longer
But the day was passing fast, so out of this bliss we came
Into the clatter of America, nothing was the same.

The heat washed over me, like opening an oven door
I slowly opened my eyes and gasped at what I saw
Men, women and children all rushing to and fro
Shoppers and sellers, all shouting as they go.

I saw hairdressers, supermarkets, toy shops and clothes stores
McDonald's, cinemas, jewellery shops and sweet stores
Smells of fat, greasy chips and burgers which people ate
As they rushed home. It was getting late.

The bright dazzling colours of neon lights line the streets
Teenagers and friends out for the night start to meet
Now in this city, rock music is the sound
As we drive in our taxi over American ground.

Laura Jaques (14)
The Cheltenham Ladies' College, Cheltenham

The Family Scene

Duncan plays his trumpet,
He hasn't done it long,
But whatever he does is stupid
And he always plays it wrong.

Patrick's always goggling,
At our widescreen TV,
He always takes the remote
And never gives it to me.

Mum is always rowing,
Or chatting on the phone,
Otherwise she's shouting
In her bossy shouting tone.

My dad is always working,
He's locked up in his study
And when he's free and you want to play,
He just grunts and watches rugby.

So I guess my family's average,
That's how they are as you can see,
But when you come to the perfect one,
It just has to be me!

Stephanie Payne (12)
The Cheltenham Ladies' College, Cheltenham

The Photograph Album

You saw them once, loved them, sought to capture them,
Now their reproductions lie, glossy, ordered, half-forgotten:
An old friend - what was she called? On a beach.
A drift of leaves caught by a lancing sliver of sunshine.
A castle, broken but beautiful, stretching tall towers to an overcast sky.
Faces you almost recognise, elusive names from the
                                    depths of your memory.
Two children, sun hats proudly displayed, eating ice creams
That one your sister - could that be you?
Sharing a child's simple happiness in sand and sun,
A blurry mountain, location unknown, from several angles.
A nameless English village, nestled in some age-old valley.
A bare tree in winter, a black silhouette against the snow.
They lie as you left them, silently reproaching you for
your carelessness of memory.
Relics of the past, souvenirs of better days.
Pathetic offerings to immortality,
An eternity of frozen moments.

Hannah Lancashire (15)
The Cheltenham Ladies' College, Cheltenham

Triolet

Love is like a cold, blustery wind.
Love is like the surface of a rippling lake.
No matter how much one has sinned
Love is like a cold, blustery wind
Love can still have you pinned
Anything for love's sake.
Love is like a cold, blustery wind
Love is like the surface of a rippling lake.

Helena Shand (14)
The Cheltenham Ladies' College, Cheltenham

Owl

You think I am a bird,
I am not.
I am the night hunter
I embrace the dark, wings stretched wide.

You think I am a bird,
I am not.
I am the shadow sweeping over you in the dark
You turn and I am gone.

You think I am a bird,
I am not.
I do not hate the light
I love the dark.

You think I am feathers, a beak
Two eyes and two claws.

I am a machine
I am designed to be the swiftest
A fleeting image
In the ebony light.
I am a hunter,
Sudden and unexpected
Shrewd and knowing
Reclusive and solitary in my ways.

You think I am a bird,
I am not.

Rosie Macfarlane (14)
The Cheltenham Ladies' College, Cheltenham

The Bat

Amongst the stalagmites and stalactites,
The cool black lakes hidden underneath the low, jagged
roofs of the cave.
The drip, drip, drip of the water
And the still, forgotten eeriness of silence,
Hanging upside down its small, scratchy claws clutched
around the tiny spikes of rock protruding out of the damp
walls of the cave.
Sleeping here, the bat, its small sensitive nostrils
flare in the darkness as it hears the scurrying of
a mouse and takes flight.

Its large clawed wings unfold and its small furry body
is chilled as it soars through the air.
Uncovered by the cloak which surrounds it by day,
keeping its small body warm as it sleeps.
It smells the fresh night-time air as it senses
its fellow friends smelling and listening.
It hears the scratch and the scurry of feet
against the cold grassy ground now being covered by a
soft blanket of dew.
Then, a race to the scurrying,
Frantic screeching and fighting.
The bat's tiny claws clamp around the squirming body of
the small furry creature,
No hope against the red-eyed, clawed, winged Dracula.

Emily Younger (14)
The Cheltenham Ladies' College, Cheltenham

Moroccan Woman

I stop and freeze,
mesmerized by those eyes,
green-grey on a dark weather-worn face.
She disappears around a corner
in to a doorway.
I wonder,
what does she do behind that
ornate door?
But wait,
there again,
sweeping black cloth,
sandals thumping softly
on the cobbles.
How does she do it?
Living life as a silent shadow puppet,
flitting like a moth,
noiseless,
just another person in the street.

Rosie McBurney (12)
The Cheltenham Ladies' College, Cheltenham

Night Intends To Stay

Earth and gravestones to honour the dead
and weapons to protect the living,
caves and clothes secreted away
and silence for days on end,
you'd need sticks to mark the weeks on trees
and stones to spark the fire
memories of how things used to be
for night intends to stay.

Imogen Bexfield (14)
The Cheltenham Ladies' College, Cheltenham

Ode To Scotland

I have not spent an hour,
On your misty shores,
But I belong to you,
Like a phoenix to its flame.

Lullaby of sea and Skye,
Sung to dreaming bairn;
Stories of my ancient past,
Dancing tunes of one great song.

Eternal, constant haze,
Evergreen and grey.
Rocky shores and purple moors;
Osprey calls to me of home.

And when I return to you,
I will belong.
Finally contented,
At one, with your great song.

Sarah Tallett-Williams (15)
The Cheltenham Ladies' College, Cheltenham

Demeter

A mother's love will never tear apart
Though the tears I weep wash the world away,
The revenge I feel takes hold in my heart,
To avenge my daughter cruelly lost one day.
Cruel winds and bitter ice to Earth I send,
No spring will be born in my freezing burn
No earthborn man against me shall defend
Till my heart is warmed by her sweet return
Six months for six months her life we divide,
Six months the Earth harvests my bitter seed,
Men pay for Hades' theft of spring's fresh bride
So for her return and for spring they plead
Earth thrives and blooms to welcome her coming,
But too soon she's gone and it shares my heart's numbing.

Sophie Simpson (15)
The Cheltenham Ladies' College, Cheltenham

A Child Is . . .

A sign of hope,
A dream come true,
An absorbment of dirt,
A song of praise,
An everlasting smile,
A grin so big,
The only thing worth living for,
Worry,
Resentment,
Happiness,
Joy,
So many emotions wrapped into one,
Their problems so big, but then again so small,
A glowing light in a dark room,
A cat and a mouse surrounded by cheese
Destruction,
Mainly they take over . . .

Sophie Devine (13)
The Cherwell School, Oxford

Do You Really Love Me?

Do you really love me
Or will you lead me on?
Please tell me the truth
Before my life is gone.

Do you really love me
Or do you want to lie?
Please baby, tell me now
'Cause right now I want to die.

Do you really love me
The gun is pointed to my head?
Sorry, you are out of time
Because right now, I'm dead . . .

Shaun Jones (14)
The Cherwell School, Oxford

Darkness Is . . .

A place where nightmares become reality,
A dark damp cave,
Where bats and vampires roam,
Horrors from your darkest secrets,
Betrayal and loneliness,
The border between life and death,
The suffocating silence,
No light, no happiness, no joy,
Into the black hole,
Slumbering deep in sleep,
Walking in the midnight streets,
One, sounds of creaking,
Two, sounds of screaming,
Three, face the nightmare of your life,
A huge claw,
Blood dripping,
An eclipse,
Memories from the beginning of life,
An unknown place,
A terrible pain,
Can't breathe,
No movement,
Death.

Susan Xia (13)
The Cherwell School, Oxford

Winter 'Love'

The snow, so peaceful and serene,
caressed by the soft moonlight,
gave magical feelings to the night.

The soft blue glow,
the lovers' words that then did flow,
their lips closer and closer
until, locked in the throes
of a passionate embrace,
he decided to express his feelings,
to keep her safe.

He whispered softly
his words like music to her ears.
'I love you,'
and her response the same,
heard like the gentle breeze,
'And I love you, forever.'

That was the night they promised
to be together through everything,
each to care for the other when old and grey
a lover's pact
the most likely to last.

Mac Tuazon (14)
The Cherwell School, Oxford

My Friends

My friends are like stars,
So treasure them dearly.
They will fade away
But they will always be there.
My friends are like raindrops,
So when there's a shower,
I will remember them for hours.
My friends are like the sun
Always there to brighten up my day
When I am down
To take away my frown.
My friends' names
Are engraved in gold
In bold
In the centre of my heart
Forever and ever!

Emma England (13)
The Neale-Wade Community College, March

Watching

I watch the millions of crosses in a row
I watch the bright red poppies in Flanders fields grow
I watch the people lay their wreaths with a sigh
I watch and as they salute, I start to cry

I see the crumbling stonework carved with names
I know that terrible war is the one to blame
I hear the gunshots ringing through my ears
Their bitter sound has brought so many tears

I watch the unmarked grave, it pains my heart
As I think of those men it tears my soul apart
Those soldiers were my friends, brave, happy, kind
And as I watch that grave from Heaven, I know it's mine.

Kimberley Wheeler (14)
The Neale-Wade Community College, March

The Process

A stone-cold bullet pierced the innocent soul
Blood came rushing out of the wrongly accused hole.
The bullet went deeper, not by his choice
Pain and horror had deserted the man's voice
He wept, he cried, at the pain he did face
The torture prolonged, slowly decreasing his pace
He fell to the floor on his hands and knees bare
Turned over on his back and remained laying there.

As the deadly round weapon lay in his lung
His body gave up, his last word sung.
His eyes dilated and his skin so pale
No sound of breathing, no painful wail.
His heartbeat slower as each minute passed
Each cell in his body was decaying fast.
His limbs remained paralysed in the sodden world
His blood leaked out, yet his mind still swirled.

He thought of his childhood, simply playing games
He thought of all the times he was ever called names
He remembered his first love and how good it feeled
He experienced again the contract he sealed.
Thinking of the time he held his own flesh and blood
Playing games with them in the wet mud
He wished he could see them for one last word
But the voices of chaperones he had then heard.

No movement of body, mind or heart
His life finally over from end to start
With no life, no soul, where could he be?
He lay there staring, so careless and free
On the cold stone bed
He lay there, lifeless and dead.

Emily Allington (13)
The Neale-Wade Community College, March

The Forest

The forest was no longer pale,
Each heartbeat could be the last,
All it needed was a lifesaver,
To inhale the ending of life.

The sweet air and warm sun,
Now only little rain,
The forest becoming enhanced,
Green leaves yet again.

Fairies arose from far around,
Flying, swirling,
Only wings making a sound.
This would be the forest's answer,
To its dead and gloomy factor,
Now once again,
People would flock in,
Leaps, jumps and bounds.

Keely Tizzard (14)
The Neale-Wade Community College, March

Why?

Why were we put on this Earth?
Why do we breathe?
Why do we long for love?
Why do we need?

Why is life so complicated?
Why is life so mean?
Why is no one ever perfect?
Why are we so keen . . .

To spend our money on everything?

Nicole Dudley (13)
The Neale-Wade Community College, March

Teacher's Pet

I hate the teacher's pet
He's in every top set
He tries to be in lead
But there's really no need
He tries to act cool
But looks like a fool
He tries to fit in
But ends up in the bin
He is such a freak
And a really big geek
His teeth are in braces
And his shoes have laces
His tie is at the top
And his hair looks like a mop
That's why we don't get
On with the teacher's pet!

Paige Dawkes (12) & Lauren Jordan (13)
The Neale-Wade Community College, March

My Name

My name is really hard to say,
I get teased about it every day.
I don't see what the problem is,
It's all the rage in showbiz.

My mum and dad make me mad,
As they made my name so bad.
My name is so original,
It's *religional*.

My friends all say,
They're going to the bay,
But I wasn't invited,
So I had to stay.

Abbie Mills & Natalie Ogden
The Neale-Wade Community College, March

The Grey Mist

The grey mist unfurled
Along the smoky sky.
Screams pierced silence
As worried faces passed me by.

Gunshots sounded in the distance
I still had a long way to go.
A shot was fired far ahead
To miss the bullet I ducked down low.

Soldiers trudged past, holding rifles
Running fast, I stumbled.
I quickly got to my feet and saw an old man
'Run, escape, quickly,' he mumbled.

I got to the border to escape into the forest
I couldn't wait to leave this terrible sight.
All of a sudden it was quiet as a mouse
Turning around I saw a bright white light.

I knew what this meant
The attack over, the evil dead.
I ran back to the city and heard everyone cheer
Across my face a thin smile spread.

Hayley Auffret (14)
The Neale-Wade Community College, March

I Hate Poems!

I hate writing poems,
They get on my nerves,
But Miss Moody,
Makes us do them in curves.

Long ones, short ones,
Maybe middle-sized,
She makes us do tons,
About great big thighs.

Poem this, poem that,
She goes on and on,
About rat-a-tat-tat,
And she always tries to con.

Some have to rhyme,
But then again, some don't,
They have to be done by a certain time,
If we ask her to listen - she won't!

So this is why I hate writing poems,
It makes me shiver,
Just because of Moody Miss Em,
And it hurts my liver!

Amy Edwards & Nicole Oliver (13)
The Neale-Wade Community College, March

Love Or Hate

I hate the way she bullies me,
The way she always shouts,
I hate the way she dobs me in,
And she bosses me about.

I love the way she's always sweet,
Like a little lamb's bleat,
I love the way she's kind and caring,
The way she's always giving and sharing.

I hate the way she always moans,
The way she always groans,
I hate the way she always tells,
The way she always yells.

I love the way she helps me,
The way she does my hair,
I love the way she gives good looks,
But not the way she stares.

Overall I love her lots,
Even though she's annoying,
Maybe next time she might be kind,
Or carry on destroying.

Kelly Green & Lindsey Harley (12)
The Neale-Wade Community College, March

Death - WW2

The fall of many men,
Missed by many at home.
The destruction falling,
Clouding the sky.

Destruction brings hope,
Hope of survival.
The growing of flowers,
Flowers of death.

Deep, dark trenches, full of fear,
Fear of what you'd see next.
The sight of your soldiers,
Soldiers lying dead.

The soldiers fighting for us,
Ready to kill.
They stand there brave and strong,
Knowing death is near.

Layla Tomsett (12)
The Neale-Wade Community College, March

Mates!

I love all my mates,
I'll treasure them forever,
Whatever the size, whatever the colour,
I don't care what they look like,
I'll dump them never!
So listen up,
All you lot out there,
This is no fake,
I'll stand by you whatever it takes,
And if I die before you do,
I'll go to Heaven . . .
And wait for you!

Christina Fisher (13)
The Neale-Wade Community College, March

Family

Family, family, family,
Whatever can it be?
Someone to love and care,
But they can be very unfair!
Brothers are the worst,
They always put themselves first!
Sisters - they're not always shy,
They always tend to lie!
They give you the little wink and smile,
It's really rather vile!
Mothers are very bossy,
Although their hair is very glossy!
Fathers are always at work,
They always wear their best shirt!
Family, family, family,
That's what's real to me.

Laura Neale
The Neale-Wade Community College, March

Split?

Last night it was over between me and Nelly,
I was so upset, he broke my heart.
I was so shocked, it was going so well,
But now we are apart.
I wish he would change his mind,
And take me back forever,
And ever and ever and evermore.

Why did I split up with Ellie?
I wish I could turn back the time!
I don't know why I did it,
It's the first thing that came into my mind.
I want her to be mine again.
I hope she is feeling the same way.

Brodie Adamson & Katie Hunter (13)
The Neale-Wade Community College, March

Rainbow

The fluorescent stripes arced high in the sky
Dashes of rose, dashes of violet
Like an artist gone mad on a canvas of blue
It's like jumping through chameleon scales.

Stripes of red, blue and orange
Arcs of green, pink and violet
Dashes of yellow and indigo on the great canvas.

I look up and see
Anger, tranquillity and sunshine
I see mould, embarrassment and strength
I visualise happiness and hope.

The little leprechauns sliding down, down, down
Just for glee and their joy
Avoiding the reaching, hoping hands
And manoeuvring out of their grasp
Anything to avoid being caught.

Their wee little hats
And snow-white beards
Their cheeky smiles
And pearly teeth,
Shining, satisfied they haven't been caught.

The arcs slowly fade
Children remember the fun they had
Waiting, just waiting
For the next one to come.

Rhianna Wells (12)
The Neale-Wade Community College, March